CORY ASBURY

Reckless Love

CHARISMA
HOUSE

Visit the author's website at coryasbury.com.

Library of Congress Cataloging-in-Publication Data:
An application to register this book for cataloging has been submitted to the Library of Congress.
International Standard Book Number: 978-1-62999-757-5
E-book ISBN: 978-1-62999-758-2

People named in this book are composites created by the author. Any similarity to the names or details of individuals known to readers is purely coincidental.

20 21 22 23 24—987654321
Printed in the United States of America

To my wife, Anna — you are the love of my life and every good thing about me. I love you more than words can tell.

To my four beautiful children, Gabriel, Lily, River, and Willow-Grace — I adore you. You make me smile every day, and I am so proud of each one of you, no matter what.

And to all the sons and daughters searching for the reckless love of the Father — you are not alone.

Before I spoke a word, You were singing over me
You have been so, so good to me
Before I took a breath, You breathed Your life in me
You have been so, so kind to me

O, the overwhelming, never-ending, reckless love of God
O, it chases me down, fights 'til I'm found, leaves the ninety-nine
I couldn't earn it, I don't deserve it, still You give Yourself away
O, the overwhelming, never-ending, reckless love of God

When I was Your foe, still Your love fought for me
You have been so, so good to me
When I felt no worth, You paid it all for me
You have been so, so kind to me

There's no shadow You won't light up
Mountain You won't climb up, coming after me
There's no wall You won't kick down
Lie You won't tear down, coming after me

O, the overwhelming, never-ending, reckless love of God

CONTENTS

SECTION III: GETTING TO THE HEART OF THE MATTER

SECTION IV: NOBODY SAID IT WAS EASY

SECTION V: ANSWERING THE CALL

FOREWORD

*O*NE OF THE major themes conveyed throughout the Bible is God's love for humanity. After all, the Bible contains the greatest love story ever told. Woven within its pages are stories of various accounts of God's extravagant love on display—a love that showed no constraint in His pursuit of the object of His affection.

I love the term *reckless*. By definition it refers to the lack of consideration concerning the consequences of one's actions. At first glance this could seem careless. But upon further review, that clearly depicts God's love—for He willingly laid His life down for us at His own expense, an act that can often be labeled reckless!

Our pursuits identify our priorities—because ultimately you'll pursue what you value. With that in mind it's evident that our value to God is unfathomable—for He loved the world so much that He gave Jesus as a ransom for us. And nothing can separate us from His love.

Early in my walk with God I received a revelation of God's love that has been the wind in my sails. One day while I was driving, I heard Jesus whisper to my heart, "John, do you know I esteem you more important than Myself?"

Initially I brushed it off as blasphemous, reasoning that God would not have said something like that to me. But as I pondered those words, I realized God had spoken to me. At the time, I was new to the faith, and I needed clarity. So I responded, "Lord, this is too extreme for me to believe. It seems blasphemous that You, Lord Jesus, would consider me more important than Yourself. The only way I can accept such a thought is if You give me three New Testament scriptures to prove it."

Without delay the Lord replied, "What does Philippians 2:3 say?"

Because I was familiar with this verse, I could quote it out loud: "Let nothing be done through selfish ambition or conceit, but in lowliness of mind let each esteem others better than himself" (NKJV).

The Lord asserted, "You have your first scripture."

Being analytical by nature—and a little stubborn—I argued, "Lord, that's Paul speaking to the Philippian believers, instructing them to esteem others better than themselves. That is not referring to Your relationship with me."

Undisturbed by my probing, God kindly clarified, "Son, I never tell My children to do anything I don't do Myself!"

Side note: that's great parenting advice, because the problem in most homes is that parents are setting standards for their children that they don't hold to themselves. Selah!

Now, back to my God moment…

As I was still trying to comprehend how the Lord could esteem me better than Himself, I continued my inquiry: "Lord, that is only one scripture. I need two more."

God's response came in the form of a question: "John, who hung on the cross, you or Me?"

As my eyes teared up, I responded, "You did, Jesus."

In that moment what I knew in theory became real to me. My heart was deeply moved, and I could feel the passion in the Lord's words: "It should have been you hanging on that cross, but I bore your sins, judgment, sickness, disease, pain, and poverty. I did it because I esteem you better than Myself." (See 1 Peter 2:24.)

I wept and worshipped while I absorbed the enormity of this revelation. Then I received the third scripture, which also came to me as a question: "What does Romans 12:10 say?"

It was another familiar verse that I quoted: "Be kindly affectionate to one another with brotherly love, in honor giving preference to one another" (NKJV).

And yes, once again the Lord affirmed, "Am I not the first-born of many brethren? I prefer and esteem my brothers and sisters better than Myself."

For several minutes I sat there speechless while I was overcome by God's presence. All my doubts receded like the tide to the sea.

Every child of God must have a revelation of God's love for him or her. It's absolutely foundational to our walk with God. My friend Cory has written a powerful book that expounds on his song "Reckless Love," which has resonated with and ministered to millions of believers. Without a doubt God's love is indeed reckless, and Cory provides us with a glimpse into his personal journey of encountering God's reckless love—and how you too can experience that love for yourself.

Prepare to be wrecked by God's reckless love!

—JOHN BEVERE
BEST-SELLING AUTHOR AND MINISTER
COFOUNDER, MESSENGER INTERNATIONAL

ACKNOWLEDGMENTS

First and foremost, my sweet Anna-Belle, I could not have done this without you. Thank you for loving me even when I don't deserve it. Your kindness has made me a better man. This book and any earthly success I might have is because of your love. Thank you for reopening the windows of my heart.

Gabriel, Lily, River, and Willow-Grace, you made me a daddy and showed me, in a way I never thought possible, what the Father's love is really like. None of these words would have been written without the gift of your lives. Thank you for reopening the eyes of my soul.

Caleb, you and I both know this book wouldn't exist without you. Thank you for helping me write it. Thank you for your hard work and dedication even in the midst of one of the most difficult seasons of your life. I won't forget it.

Mom and Dad, I love you both so much. Thanks for always believing in me and pouring into me. I know there have been some bumps along the road, but I've never questioned for even one second how much you both love me and how proud of me you are. Thank you for your sacrifices. They were—and are—the stepping stones to where I am today.

Summer and David, your friendship is everything. The belly laughs, late-night cry sessions, and heartfelt conversations shared with you guys have shaped who we are and kept us steady when we wanted to quit. Thank you for always being there for us no matter what. We love you.

Introduction

FROM BETHEL TO BIEBER
(AND EVERYTHING IN BETWEEN)

WHEN I WROTE "Reckless Love," I had no idea it would go on to be one of the most popular Christian songs in recent history. I had no idea it would go viral in a matter of hours after hitting YouTube. I had no idea it would break Billboard records and receive numerous Dove awards and even a Grammy nomination. I had no idea it would become the most frequently sung worship song in the church worldwide; no idea that its "theology" would be so hotly debated and the "controversy" surrounding its lyrics would galvanize the internet to create a myriad of (hilarious) memes. And I *definitely* never imagined those same lyrics would inspire tattoos on peoples' bodies. I just knew they were exactly what my heart needed to sing to the Father in that particular season of my life.

When I sent the demo to my (now) manager at Bethel Music, I included the note, "I think I just penned my opus." While I had no idea my "opus" would be so widely received, I knew it was born from the depths of my being, from the very core of my raw, imperfect-but-beautiful walk with the Father.

At that point in my life, I was so hyper-acquainted with my own brokenness that the reality of God's desire and love for me even in that vulnerable place was absolutely wrecking me (in the best way possible). He kept showing up at the doorstep of my heart when I least expected it: after another loss in the battle against lust, after blowing up at my kids (undoubtedly over something inconsequential), after yet another fight with my wife (in which I was undeniably in the wrong). It seemed as if I just couldn't outrun His grace and I couldn't "outfall" His kindness. In that place of surrender to His goodness, the refrain of the chorus was born: "O, the overwhelming, never-ending, reckless love of God." These words were the banner over my very existence.

Isn't it just like God to use a season like mine to birth a song that heals a multitude? Isn't it just like God to turn disappointments into dance floors? He really is better than we've imagined. I'm constantly overwhelmed by His tenderness in my life.

I've received literally tens of thousands of emails and messages about how the song has touched people's lives. One of my favorite testimonies came on the day Justin Bieber sang the song on his social media platforms. Boy, did my phone blow up that day. I was inundated with messages from friend and foe alike excitedly telling me that Bieber had sung my song. To be honest with you, I completely freaked out too. I didn't expect to be so giddy and starstruck, but I was. That day, I received thousands of messages from random people who had heard the song because of Justin's posts. The one that impacted me the most came from a young man who was planning on committing suicide that very night. When he heard Justin singing the words to my song, the Father came close and spoke sonship and belonging over him. He gave his life to God that very day and was saved. It's amazing what Jesus can do with just a little tune, huh?

So, as you read the words and stories in this book, I pray that you too will encounter the wildness of God's love. I pray that His reckless pursuit of your heart will cause you to lay down all your defenses and preconceived notions of who He is. I pray that with every new day of this forty-day journey, you'll see Him more clearly and experience His love more deeply. May His smile be your portion and His affection your fuel.

PROFILE OF A LOVING GOD

IS GOD'S LOVE RECKLESS?

The French Easter liturgy says, "L'amour de Dieu est
folie"—the love of God is foolishness. And Jesus says
it is a foolishness that is meant to call forth joy.
—BRENNAN MANNING

I'VE BEEN ASKED countless times how and why I would
choose to use a word like *reckless* to describe the love
of God. Some "critics" have been gracious, and some have
been less than gracious (to put it lightly). While I understand
that my choice of words is undoubtedly bold, I believe in a
God whose love is infinitely beyond the bounds of our English
Rolodex of descriptors, a God who lives so far outside the
confines of human language that words fail to describe even
the edges of His complexity.

At the height of the controversy surrounding the song in
2018, it seemed as if its opponents made it their goal to disprove the idea of God's reckless love. I can't tell you how many
internet blogs, news articles, and social media posts tagged
me in their publications. Looking at it in retrospect, I believe
most people who took offense at the word fall into two main
camps. (I'm sure there are other groups with considerably
more nuance, but these two are the biggies.)

People in the first camp hold the notion that nothing can
happen outside God's foreknowledge (since He's omniscient);
therefore, none of His actions could ever be deemed reckless. These people would call Jesus' death on the cross "calculated" and "intentional." I would offer this rebuttal: Jesus
knew that Lazarus would rise again in John 11, yet He still

wept for Him. Why? Because omniscience (or precognition) doesn't negate the pain of the foreseen event. In other words, just because you know something painful is going to happen in the future doesn't mean it's not going to hurt when it does.

We must remember, Jesus was fully God *and* fully man, which means, like us, He carried the capacity for deep emotion—empathy, sadness, sorrow, and suffering. Describing the cross as calculated because it was always part of His plan doesn't make it any less grueling. It would be like knowing you are going to the dentist tomorrow to get a root canal—without anesthesia. Just because you've got it on the calendar doesn't mean it's not going to hurt like crazy. So while the adjectives *calculated* and *intentional* are certainly true of our Savior's work at Calvary, they don't intrinsically preclude the application of the word *reckless*. In other words, someone could be "intentionally reckless." Allow me to illustrate this idea in two analogies.

In the first a father named Richard plans to surprise his son, Jesse, with the gift of a lifetime: a brand-new car for his sixteenth birthday. For the sake of making this illustration more relatable (and more dramatic), let's say this car is a red Lamborghini Aventador S. This model retails for almost half a million dollars, but hey, Richard really loves his son, you know?

At first glance, do you as an outside observer think it is wise of Richard to give his son such an expensive vehicle at such a young age? Do you think it's a sensible thing to do?

I suggest that, in light of what we know about the general temperament of most teenagers, it is not sensible. Plus, the latest data tells us the leading cause of teen death is accidental injuries, such as car-crash injuries.[1] Perhaps the 740-horsepower engine of the Lamborghini might tempt Jesse to drive a little faster than the speed limit one night. What if he gets careless with his friends and loses his life in a tragic accident? Was the car a wasted gift? Was it just a foolish gesture? Again, I'd like to suggest that it was not.

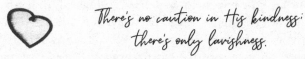

There's no caution in His kindness; there's only lavishness.

You see, God doesn't give gifts according to our ability to steward them perfectly or our worthiness to receive them. Neither did the father in this story. God gives according to one criterion—His ridiculous kindness. He hands out good gifts left and right like it is Christmas morning all year round, because it's just who He is. It's His nature; He cannot be any other way. His character is overflow. There's no caution in His kindness; there's only lavishness.

Our second illustration examines one of God's greatest gifts to humanity: the gift of children. In this scenario a newly married young couple, James and Rachel, just found out they're pregnant with their first child—a little boy. Sadly James isn't as excited as he should be at the news. You see, he was sexually abused as a child and still hasn't found the courage to tell his wife. The shame of his prior experience clouds his ability to feel the hope and joy that should accompany such a mountaintop moment. He's scared, and rightly so. Bringing a child into this world is a weighty thing. James worries that he's going to fall into the unfortunate patterns of his childhood and end up hurting his son.

Now let's ponder something. Is it foolish for God to allow James—a broken, sinful human being with a less-than-perfect past—to bring a child into this world? Probably. I mean, if anyone is acquainted with humanity's propensity for darkness, it's Almighty God. Yet He affords James the gift of a child anyway because He's just that good.

Is there not a strong possibility that James might affect the life of his little boy in a negative way? Absolutely. But what if God in His infinite wisdom knows this is a divine opportunity for healing and redemption? What if God knows this is where the power of the cross can purify James' past and send his shame packing once and for all? What if becoming a dad could somehow heal the scars of his childhood? Did God think through the vast number of outcomes for this father-son relationship? Has He predestined it, or does James have a choice in the matter?

I believe James has a choice, and his choice is the canvas on which to display his gratitude for God's "foolish" gift, His intentionally reckless display of love. Therein lies the beauty of the entire equation of life: God lets us choose how we'll respond to His preposterous mercy, to His scandalous grace. Almost overlooked amid all the trappings of the Father's generosity, our free will might be the greatest and most reckless gift of all.

This leads to our second camp of opponents: those who say God's love can't be reckless because their associations with the word *reckless* are negative. In other words, since the word typically carries negative connotations, it can't be ascribed to God because He's altogether positive. Consider this: Scripture says that God is a jealous God; yet "Thou shalt not covet" (Exod. 10:17, KJV) is one of the Ten Commandments. How can this "paradox" be? The answer is, word association does not equal word definition. Preconceived notions of a word—positive or negative—do not determine that word's function or meaning.

The idea that God could be reckless in His pursuit of humanity also threw many people off. They felt it implied that

He needed our affection in return (and obviously the God who has everything doesn't need anything). In their estimation this notion painted God as weak, whiny, whimpering, and love-scorned. It made Him look needy, and most Christians (especially those only outwardly familiar with the Jesus of the Bible) prickle at this notion, because to them, God is only ever big, strong, and barrel-chested. But God—yes, the same God who created heaven and earth—gives Himself away in desperate hopes that we'll return His love. He is that vulnerable and humble, and His heart is that tender.

It's not weakness as many misperceive. God's longing to be loved isn't a suspension of His power; it's evidence of the incomprehensible fury of His love. A. W. Tozer says it like this: "[God] waits to be wanted."[2] He's not a sad schoolgirl wallowing like a wallflower at the high school dance; He's a Father, fierce in love, coming after His sons and daughters with reckless abandon.

To support the second camp's position that a negative word can't characterize God, a lot of articles and blog posts cited synonyms for *reckless* in an attempt to discredit the song. They cherry-picked the words that served their purpose while neglecting the others. The inexactness of this logic is quite shocking. It reminds me of arguments I often see on social media (usually between Christians and non-Christians), in which the debaters pick and choose which scriptures they want to use as ammunition for their empty squabbles, regardless of the actual context of the verses.

Just for fun, here are a few synonyms for *reckless* using the same (dubious) method:

• adventuresome	• carefree	• headlong
• adventurous	• daring	• wild
• audacious		

Here are a few antonyms:

- afraid
- careful
- cautious
- discreet
- fearful
- reserved
- shy
- timid
- wary

I don't know about you, but I don't serve a God who's anything close to afraid, fearful, shy, timid, or reserved. My God is wild, full of life, and much more like a lion than a domesticated cat.

This exercise demonstrates that our vocabulary is too limited to describe an ineffable God, a mysterious God who lives outside of time and space. The God who created the cosmos and its languages cannot be contained within their constructs. We seek words that fall infinitely short of the Creator of the universe. Yet as writers and artists we still have a responsibility to make Him known, both as descriptively and as precisely as possible. Our language is too feeble, yet we must try. We find ourselves smack-dab in the middle of a glorious quandary. God is too wonderful for prose, too beautiful for poetry, and too brilliant for love songs. He is altogether indescribable. Lifetimes could be wasted trying to create something worthy of His incomparable splendor, and they would be wasted most nobly.

My friend Glenn Packiam said it best: "The point of using the word *reckless* is that it shows us that by all accounts God's loving us was not what we'd call a wise investment. We were a risk, even a waste. Yet He loved us anyway. New Testament scholar, John Barclay calls this 'the incongruity of grace'—God's love for us is not congruent with our worth or our state. So, from conventional wisdom, it is reckless. A reckless use of money is to give an inheritance to someone who squanders it; it's to give a feast to someone who deserves to starve; it's to give a robe and a ring to someone who should be wearing a ball and chain. But the wisdom of God is foolishness to the world. And the foolishness of God is wiser than the wisdom of the world. Thanks be to God!"[3]

Going Deeper

Today you read about the controversy surrounding my use of the word *reckless*. I explained how, in my view, God's love is reckless, and that's a wonderful thing.

+ Think back to the first time you heard "Reckless Love." What was your emotional reaction to the words? Did you feel any pushback against the word *reckless*? Why or why not?

+ As you read my description of God's reckless love, what deepened your understanding of God's love for you? Which insight left you wanting to explore His love more?

+ If you could draw a picture that represented how you feel about God's reckless love, what would it look like?

> For the foolishness of God is wiser than human wisdom, and the weakness of God is stronger than human strength.
>
> —1 Corinthians 1:25, niv

Father, open my understanding to the reckless nature of Your love. Help me grasp and enjoy the wildness of Your love. Your indescribable love for me drove Jesus to the cross. Fill me with everything I need to respond back to You with reckless love. Your love for me pales against any other affection. Let my love for You do the same.

Day 2

WHAT LOVE LOOKS LIKE

Agape…is a love that seeks nothing in return. It is an overflowing love; it's what theologians would call the love of God working in the lives of men. And when you rise to love on this level, you begin to love men, not because they are likeable, but because God loves them.
—MARTIN LUTHER KING, JR.

I'VE OFTEN WONDERED what would've been written about me if I had been one of Jesus' twelve disciples. Which quotes would the Gospels have ascribed to me? In most of my ponderings, they're not exactly canon worthy. Stupid questions such as, Do animals go to heaven? and Why can't penguins fly? are often the fodder of my less-than-focused quiet times nowadays. So my guess is, even with Jesus directly in front of me in the flesh, my musings wouldn't be any nobler.

If I were to identify with any of the disciples, it would have to be Peter. He was always blurting out the stupid things everybody else was thinking (but not saying) and chopping people's ears off. He was the type of guy who thought he had it all together, the guy who would finish his test first in class and proudly walk to the front of the room to turn it in so everybody noticed, the guy who would eagerly raise his hand when the teacher asked a question, whether he knew the answer or not. Granted, Peter did get a few things right. By revelation, he accurately described Jesus as "the Christ, the son of the living God" (Matt. 16:16) when others doubted. Peter went on to become an essential figure in the New Testament church, and Jesus even called him the "rock" upon which the Christian church would be built (Matt. 16:18).

Then came Peter's tragic downfall. Like many great historical Greek figures Peter was brought down by hubris, an extreme and excessive sense of pride and self-confidence. After swearing on his life that he would never deny Jesus, Peter was one of the first to betray Him. In his enthusiastic arrogance he believed himself to be unshakable. But following three vehement denials of Christ, Peter was more than shaken; he was probably totally shattered on the inside.

I believe Peter is a case study in one of Jesus' main principles from the Sermon on the Mount—a stunning illustration of Matthew 5:3: "Blessed are the poor in spirit." Oh, the brokenness Peter must have felt as the cock crowed the second time, reminding him of Jesus' fateful words (which he cavalierly rejected) in Mark 14:30, "you yourself will deny Me three times."

The disciple who always had the right answers and knew exactly what to do was suddenly stopped dead in his tracks by crippling regret. You can almost hear Peter's heart breaking as Jesus brings up the sore subject over a post-resurrection breakfast on the beach. Jesus asks, "Simon, son of John, do you love Me?" And again, "Do you love Me?" And a third time, "Do you love Me?" (John 21:15–17). With every mounting query, Peter's once-vibrant, youthful zeal wanes a little more.

I imagine Jesus repeated the question partly because Peter just sat there silently, realizing, perhaps for the first time in his life, that he honestly had no idea what to say. Finally, grieved by his own brokenness, Peter replies, "Lord, You know all things; You know that I love You" (v. 17). But it's as if his words betray his heart. I imagine the refrain of his soul was something more like, "Lord, You know all things. You know my love is weak, certainly weaker than I once imagined."

Although trials and pressures had crushed his confidence, the love Peter declared on the beach that morning was still real. More importantly the love Jesus showed Peter in asking him to tend His sheep despite his obvious flaws was equally real. The fact that Jesus still trusted Peter with His church, even after seeing his capacity for failure, says a lot more than is explicitly written in the Gospel's account.

Still, many of us think our weaknesses and failures disqualify us from God's love. However, the exact opposite is true. Now, I know what you're thinking: "How could messing up more make God love me more?" Well, that's not exactly what I'm saying. Let me explain in more detail with a quick story from Luke chapter 7.

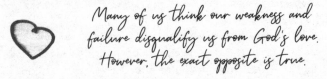

Many of us think our weakness and failure disqualify us from God's love. However, the exact opposite is true.

Here, Jesus tells a man named Simon about two people who owed money to a moneylender. One person owes five hundred dollars, and another owes fifty dollars. (It was actually denarii, but for the sake of accessibility, let's use dollars instead.)

Neither person had the money to pay the moneylender back, so he completely forgave both people their debts. What a nice guy, huh? (Spoiler alert: the moneylender is a type of Christ). Jesus then asks Simon which of them will love him more. Simon replies, "I suppose the one who had the bigger debt forgiven" (Luke 7:43, NIV). Precisely! When we realize how much we need forgiveness, our hearts explode with love for the forgiver. To paraphrase 1 John, it's not that we loved

God, but He loved us first (4:19). Only when we realize how much God loves us despite our inadequacies can we love Him rightly in return. His love is unconditional. It's not based on what we can do; it's based on who He is. And thank God, He is love.

Going Deeper

Today we looked at our own weaknesses and pride in contrast with the unconditional agape love of God. Peter is a perfect metaphor for the way our good intentions don't always match how we live life out every day.

+ **In which ways did you identify with Peter today?**

+ **Have you ever sincerely surrendered all to God while you were worshipping at church, only to blow it before you even got to the restaurant for lunch?**

+ **In the past what were some unhealthy ways you dealt with your good intentions toward God that went bad? What were some healthy ways you handled your sin?**

However grievous your latest failure might be, run to Him in repentance and let His forgiveness wipe away all the shame you're feeling. Instead of letting guilt keep you from His presence, run to Him so your gratitude born of His forgiveness will explode into praise. Believe me when I say that there's no sound louder than a captive set free. So let the redeemed of the Lord say so!

> I waited patiently for the LORD; and He inclined to me and heard my cry....He set my feet upon a rock making my footsteps firm. He put a new song in my

mouth, a song of praise to our God; many will see and fear and will trust in the Lord.

—Psalm 40:1–3

Lord, once again I come to You with my head hung down. I can't believe I did it again. Thank You, Lord, that just as You ask me to forgive people over and over, You do the same for me. I am truly grateful. Now I join with Jeremiah in pleading for You to do in me what I cannot seem to do: "Heal me, O Lord, and I will be healed; save me and I will be saved, for You are my praise" (Jer. 17:14). I trust You with this. I receive Your forgiveness, and I forgive myself. Thank You for Your agape love.

EITHER HE'S GOOD, OR HE ISN'T

Our faith can only go as far as our awareness of God's goodness.
—BILL JOHNSON

I N THE LATE fall of 2013 our first daughter arrived. Lily Joy Asbury was born weighing six pounds even, perfectly healthy in every way. Anna and I were immediately smitten. She was the most beautiful thing we'd ever beheld, and from the moment we saw her, she captured our hearts completely. Her bright blonde hair and sky-blue eyes were a pleasant surprise for our entire family, as most of us (extended and immediate family) have dark complexions and dark eyes. Her beauty was unique and truly cherished by all who met her. I remember rocking her back and forth as I sang prophetically over her each night before bed. I would declare truth and destiny over her with new songs each evening. It felt as if she completed our little family.

Everything changed about three months later when Lily had her first of many life-threatening seizures. It was very early one morning when Anna violently shook me awake, screaming, "She's not breathing, Cory! She's not breathing!"

My body rose in a shell-shocked, zombie-like state as I tried to make sense of what was happening. "Call 9-1-1!" I blurted out without even thinking about it. Before we had time to process what was happening, Anna (in her pajama shorts and without a coat on a blizzard-like winter morning) grabbed Lily's limp, pale body, jumped into her 4Runner, and headed to the hospital about four minutes from our house. Thank God she took matters into her own hands, because it was another fifteen to twenty minutes before the ambulance reached our home, and who knows whether Lily's infant body would've lasted that long without medical intervention.

Trying frantically to process what was happening, I woke Gabriel (our then four-year-old) and rushed to the hospital. When I got there, they were still trying to resuscitate Lily on an operating table. Gabriel burst out crying, scared and confused; I quickly followed his lead. It was one of the scariest moments of our lives. We all watched in disbelief as doctors worked to revive her. As a dad the feeling of helplessness was devastating. There was nothing I could do to fix my baby girl. All I could do was watch and pray (in tongues, very loudly).

My mind immediately began to wander to the darkest places. Is Lily going to die? Will she ever be the same? What have I done to offend God? Why would He take my baby away from me? What deep, dark sin have I committed to stir God's anger against my family? Is. this. my. fault? It's funny how a crisis instantly crumbles all the typical walls and barriers that keep you from thinking thoughts as hopeless as these.

A few days later, after what felt like a lifetime, Lily was discharged from the hospital. Unfortunately the doctors weren't able to give us any conclusive answers as to why this had happened to Lily, so we left confused, distraught, and defeated. For the first few weeks following the incident, we pretended it hadn't shaken us to the core. We ignored the intense pain and soul-crushing questions that constantly barraged our minds. It wasn't until it happened again (and again and again and again) that I truly wrestled with the question: Is God good, or is He not?

Allow me to provide some levity amid a pretty heavy story. Eventually we took Lily to a neurologist where we discovered that these episodes were cyanotic spells (which is a fancy way of saying she held her breath until she passed out in response to intense pain). We realized the common thread was an antibiotic she had been taking. An allergic reaction to the antibiotic had caused her throat to swell and hurt. Then, because her little brain and body didn't know how to respond to the pain and trauma of the swelling, she would hold her breath and pass out. Lily is 100 percent healthy today. She is strong and happy and has not suffered an episode for almost two years. Though we did eventually figure it out, the years of uncertainty in between were still tumultuous.

It's easy to love and trust God when life is good, but when things fall apart is when we find out what we truly believe. I grew up saying things such as, "God is good! All the time!" But in this time of testing, I realized I didn't actually believe those words. They were just nice ideas that kept me feeling safe and secure. They weren't planted in me deep enough to get me through this season. Instead I had to dig down and honestly look at whether I had faith in God's goodness. I threw out all of the stock, customary answers entrenched in my mind—whether from Sunday school or random religious rhetoric I'd picked up along the way—and grappled with the very real questions I had concerning His character (or in my mind, His lack thereof).

It's easy to love and trust God when life is good, but when things start to fall apart, that's when we find out what we truly believe.

In my anger and confusion I screamed and yelled things like, "God, if You're so good, how come You're letting Lily suffer like this?! If You're so powerful, why don't You just heal her?! If You're such a good provider, why are our medical bills piling up?!" (Full disclosure: there were probably some more "colorful" words strewn in there). To my surprise God answered. He didn't have to, and the way I was asking sure didn't merit a response. But He answered anyway.

I'm not going to force-feed you the things He spoke to my heart in that season like some sort of one-size-fits-all panacea to your problems, because I believe He wants to speak to each of us individually. But I do want to encourage you on your journey. I'm sure many of you find yourselves in places similar to what I just described. Your problem might not be health-related, but maybe it's financial distress, marital difficulties, a wayward child, problems in the workplace, discord within the church, or something else. We face myriad trials as humans, and every one of them is intended to turn us toward Him in trust instead of away from Him in offense.

I imagine that after a whirlwind of destruction wreaked havoc on Job's entire family and life, he had many reasons to be offended at God. Yet he kept his heart open and allowed Yahweh to work in him "an eternal weight of glory" (2 Cor. 4:17) that no man could take from him. That, I believe, is the point of all of this.

James puts it best in the first chapter of his best (and only) epistle: "Consider it all joy, my brethren, when you encounter various trials, knowing that the testing of your faith produces endurance. And let endurance have its perfect result, so that you may be perfect and complete, lacking in nothing" (Jas. 1:2–4).

Count it joy. The hard stuff of life is like the h
sure that produce diamonds, like the irritant tha.
self-defense, coats with nacre to produce the pearl. Gross, I
know, but the point is, you don't get beauty without a little bit
of ugly. So say yes to the invitation to grow in maturity and
relationship with Jesus even when it hurts.

Going Deeper

I like the way Bill Johnson puts it: "God is good, and He is a
perfect Father. His goodness is beyond our ability to comprehend, but not our ability to experience. Our hearts will take
us where our heads can't fit."[1] God is truly good.

But perhaps you, too, have had an experience that shattered your platitudes and caused you to wrestle with God.
Maybe you dug deep at that time and resolved it. Or maybe
now is the time to do that.

- Describe an experience that caused your beliefs about God
  to feel hollow. How did you respond? What was the eventual
  outcome?

- What was most valuable to you during this time? What
  helped you the most?

- How did coming out on the other side of this experience
  strengthen your relationship with God?

You don't need to fear coming to God with your honest
feelings and questions. A faith that is tried is a stronger faith.

> So be truly glad. There is wonderful joy ahead, even
> though you must endure many trials for a little while.
> These trials will show that your faith is genuine. It is
> being tested as fire tests and purifies gold—though

your faith is far more precious than mere gold. So when your faith remains strong through many trials, it will bring you much praise and glory and honor on the day when Jesus Christ is revealed to the whole world.

—1 Peter 1:6–7, nlt

Father, I know that You welcome me when I come to You with questions and a disturbed heart. Thank You that You invite me in and spend time with me to get Your truth in me. You are truly a good God, and through Your strengthening, I will see Your goodness in everything I experience. Thank You for the times when my faith has been through the fire and has come out as pure gold. I want nothing more than to please You.

A NEW LENS

God loves us so much He wants to destroy
our preconceptions about Him.
—HEIDI BAKER

I
N OUR CULTURE first impressions are one of the most
important factors in making new relationships. Psychologists believe that a first impression shapes your mental picture of a person forever. Suffice it to say, the way you introduce yourself to people is hugely instrumental in how they remember you. Maybe you let them know that you prefer to go by a nickname rather than your given name. Perhaps it's important to you that people perceive you as a caring and thoughtful person, so you make sure to smile and say something kind. Whatever it may be, the first face-to-face moment you share with someone is critical in forming an understanding of that person, and vice versa.

In Exodus 34 Israel's leader, Moses, boldly requests a face-to-face introduction to the God of creation. Moses was in the midst of a national crisis. Though he was obeying God's commands, Israel had turned away from the Lord and worshipped a golden calf. Moses realized his need for a greater revelation of God in order to properly lead the people of Israel beyond this rebellion and into the glorious future the Lord had promised them.

> Moses said, "I pray You, show me Your glory!" And
> He said, "I Myself will make all My goodness pass
> before you, and will proclaim the name of the LORD
> before you."
> —EXODUS 33:18–19

Moses undoubtedly had some preconceived notion about God's demeanor when he asked to see His face. Just days before, he had felt the heat of God's anger at Israel's idolatry. And mere years before that, he had a front-row seat to God's judgments on Egypt (and let's not forget the intensity of the final plague—death upon all the firstborns). It would only be natural for Moses to have thoughts like, "I wonder if He'll be angry? I wonder if His judgments will leave me terrified and scarred for life?" But Moses' desire to genuinely know God outweighed His fear, so he approached God with boldness, despising the potentially unfavorable consequences.

We all get an uneasy feeling when meeting someone famous or powerful for the first time. Even a simple job interview with a potential boss or talking with a local politician can trigger anxiety. What about the giddy nervousness we feel when meeting someone we've had a crush on for months? Moses must have been feeling all these things to the nth degree as he prepared to encounter the God of Genesis chapter 1! His heart must've been pounding out of his chest as he hid in the cleft of the rock! But probably to Moses' surprise the name with which God greeted him wasn't "The Lord God, angry, intense, and mean" but rather "The Lord God, merciful and gracious, longsuffering, and abounding in goodness and truth" (Exod. 34:6, NKJV).

Because the Israelites didn't know God's heart, the intensity with which He had crushed the wickedness of Pharaoh and the swiftness with which He dealt with the rebellion of Israel had created fear in their hearts. Their lack of relationship with God caused them to interpret His actions as anger instead of paternal protection. Israel lived at a distance from God because they were scared of what He might do if they

disobeyed His commands. What the Father sh
in the cleft of the rock that day is the same thi
to show us today—that His heart, the center of who He is, is
kind and compassionate.

We've all known people who appeared to be kind at first. But
as we got to know them, we discovered that the warm exte-
riors we first saw were just cheap veneers (or as Jesus called it in
Matthew 23:27, "whitewashed tombs") masking completely different and altogether malicious hearts underneath. I think we
sometimes make this same mistake concerning God. We might
know the cute little memory verses about His love, but we genuinely believe that if we get past the niceties, we'll uncover the real
truth that He's cruel and cold.

When God proclaimed His name to Moses, He wasn't just
telling him how He wanted to be perceived; He was showing
him who He really was. He was revealing His heart. Moses
glimpsed a God who was not an angry taskmaster but a kind
and patient Father. Our hearts need this same revelation. We
have the benefit of the entirety of Scripture, testimonies of
God's goodness from around the world, and most of all, the
glory of God in the face of Jesus Christ; yet we are still as
easily deceived as the people of Israel. We can all be tricked
by the enemy into believing that God isn't who He says He is
and into thinking that if He had a moment of brutal honesty
with us, He would obliterate us with His pent-up anger and
disappointment.

While we might not be melting down our jewelry to
fashion a golden calf, how often do we run to idols instead
of His presence after a fall because we're scared of His reaction? How often do we medicate with things like movies,
social media, alcohol, and even drugs? We can't cope with the

thought that the God who created us might be disappointed not just with what we've done but with who we are. This lack of understanding of His character can cause us to live at a distance from God.

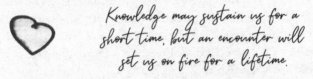

Knowledge may sustain us for a short time, but an encounter will set us on fire for a lifetime.

How can we read so many scriptures, sing so many songs, and hear so many sermons on the goodness of God yet remain unconvinced of it? I propose that it's because His kindness is, for many of us, just a concept we grasp intellectually and never encounter experientially. All the knowledge in the world doesn't compare to one real encounter with Him. Knowledge may sustain us for a short time, but an encounter will set us on fire for a lifetime.

In one momentary brush with God, Moses discovered a truth as relevant today as it was thousands of years ago: to have real relationship with God, we must have a deep understanding of His kindness as revealed through the Holy Spirit and Scripture. Until we see His goodness pass before our eyes, we may interpret the circumstances of life through a lens that sees God as angry or aloof instead of loving. We need to pray the same prayer Moses prayed: "Show me your glory!"

Going Deeper

Have you encountered God's love and kindness today? If you can't see, feel, or believe that your Father is smiling over you, I'd like to suggest that you need an encounter with His kindness.

- Close your eyes and quiet yourself enough to picture your heavenly Father. Is there a smile on His face? Or is there a scowl? Ask Him how He feels about you. Don't be afraid. Take time to write it down.

- Ask God to show you where your image of Him came from. If He reveals that someone influenced your view of Him negatively, release that image of Him and renew your mind, starting with what God said about Himself to Moses.

> The LORD God, merciful and gracious, longsuffering, and abounding in goodness and truth.
>
> —EXODUS 34:6, NKJV

We won't be able to fully trust God until we are utterly and unconditionally convinced of His kindness. Thanks be to God—He is more than eager to help us on this journey.

> *My Father, I release any images of You that don't match what Your Word says about You. As I read this week, show me Your nature and character in the stories of the Bible. I choose today to believe that You are a good and kind God who loves me and likes being with me.*

WHY HE LEAVES THE NINETY-NINE

To seek after the one and leave the ninety-nine seems so dispropor-
tionate. It seems so careless. For heaven's sake, Lord, let the silly
one go. After all, that's what he/she deserves. You've got ninety-nine
others who need your attention and care. A love that isn't "reckless"
might reason like that. But not Jesus. His love is of a different order.
—SAM STORMS

Have you ever spent time in an ER? If so, you know
how long it can take to be seen by a doctor. Sometimes it feels as if they call everyone except you. Each one
rises in hope-filled buoyancy as the nurse beckons him or her
to exam rooms of healing, youth, and prosperity while you
waste away, not knowing if your next breath will be your last.
OK, so I'm a little dramatic, but you get the point.

The truth is, we don't have it so bad nowadays. In times of
war they employed a method called triage by which patients
(especially in high-casualty areas) were examined and sorted for
treatment according to the severity of their wounds or sickness.
This method was designed to maximize the number of survi-
vors. However, the obvious implications of it are grim—some
patients would not receive the treatment they needed because
others required it more. Quiet resignation to the likelihood
that some victims were just too far gone was a decided reality.

Sometimes I can't help but think that is what Jesus was doing
during His time on earth—a sort of divine triage. He walked
the streets seeking the ones who needed His touch the most,
while the self-righteous Pharisees and Sadducees avoided Him,

thinking they did not need a Savior. How wrong they were. But thank God, no one is too far gone for His saving grace.

Let's look at the story of the ninety-nine in Luke chapter 15. For the sake of those who are unfamiliar with it, here is a quick recap. First, the context is massively significant. Scripture tells us that the scribes and Pharisees were grumbling against Jesus because He was keeping company with tax collectors and sinners, and they didn't like that. The way I picture it, the stage is set for Jesus to put the religious leaders in their place in a big way (and He doesn't disappoint).

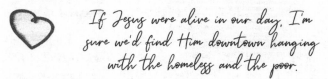

If Jesus were alive in our day, I'm sure we'd find Him downtown hanging with the homeless and the poor.

According to the CASV (Cory Asbury Standard Version), the story goes a little something like this: A man has a hundred sheep and loses one of them. Should he leave the ninety-nine in the open field to search for the one lost sheep? Absolutely! And when he finds it, he throws it over his shoulders and rejoices. When he finally gets back home, carrying his one lost sheep, he calls all his friends and neighbors together to party! In the same way, there is more joy in heaven over one lost sinner coming home than over ninety-nine righteous people who are already in the house.

One of my favorite things about Jesus is the fact that He wasn't afraid to hang out with the riffraff of Israel—the ones who absolutely did not deserve a seat at the table. If Jesus were alive in our day, I'm sure we'd find Him downtown hanging with the homeless and the poor. Although most religious people thought those folks didn't deserve Jesus' nearness, they were the exact caste of people who found themselves in close proximity to Him throughout the Gospel accounts. I suggest that He spent time with them because they actually wanted to be near Him. They understood that He had something they needed. My guess is that they weren't even sure what drew them to Him, but something about His kindness kept them following Him in droves. These were "the sick" that Jesus referred to in Mark 2.

> Jesus said to them, "It is *not* those who are healthy who need a physician, but those who are sick; I did *not* come to call the righteous, but sinners.
> —MARK 2:17, EMPHASIS ADDED

Ironically the ones in greatest need of a physician—though they didn't know it—were the religious elite of their day. That's a stark reminder that self-righteousness keeps us blinded to the beauty of grace in motion.

Jesus leaves the ninety-nine for the ones who know their need. Like blind Bartimaeus, these "ones" are often the loudest; they just won't shut up or take no for an answer, no matter who or what tries to silence them. Like the woman with the issue of blood in Matthew 9, these "ones" despise cultural norms and religious regulations that attempt to keep them in line, because their need for a cure is greater than their fear of public humiliation. Like Mary of Bethany, who anointed Jesus' feet in the middle of a room full of stuffy, religious men reclining in a post-dinner stupor, these "ones" don't care about disrupting the status quo. These "ones" cannot keep silent, because silence would relegate them to lives that are less than what Jesus paid for with His precious blood.

One of my favorite Bible stories is found in Matthew 20:1–16. I'll give you the quick CASV version. A landowner hires a bunch of workers early one morning for one hundred dollars a day. About half way through the workday, the landowner sees a bunch of other guys looking for a job. He hires them for the remainder of the day and tells them he'll pay them whatever he feels their work was worth. This happens three more times that day, with the last hire taking place just before five o'clock in the evening.

When the sun goes down, the landowner instructs his foreman to pay all the guys equally—one hundred dollars each, starting with the last ones hired and going on to the first. Now, when the guys who were first hired come to receive their wages, they expect to get more than the last guys, and they throw a fit when they only receive one hundred dollars each. So the landowner responds (in my paraphrase), "Am I being unfair? Did you not agree to work for one hundred dollars? And is not one hundred dollars what you got? What's it to you if I pay the last guys the same as you? Does my generosity anger you?"

This story is one of my favorite illustrations of the grace of God. Grace ruffles the feathers of the pietistic elite like nothing else. The self-righteous think they have to earn everything by their blood, sweat, and tears. They are offended when someone doesn't work as hard as them for a ticket to heaven but gets a "free pass" instead—someone like the sinner next to Jesus on the cross (often referred to as Dismas), who cried out for mercy in his final breaths. He was allowed into paradise that very day even though his ticket was previously punched for hell. The self-righteous scoff at the mercy shown to Dismas when they should be rejoicing with him. But it's the reckless confidence in God's goodness that compels Dismas to cry out, knowing that his feeble request might be honored by the One who holds the keys to death and the grave.

My favorite people in the world are those who have learned

to receive gifts freely, without awkwardness—especially the gift of God's grace. The truth is, it's difficult for most of us to receive. It feels like charity, and we don't like charity. Nevertheless we must learn to let Him wash our feet. In fact He said we have no part in Him if we don't allow Him to wash our feet. We must learn to cry out with the desperation of a lost sheep bleating in the thicket for its very life. There and only there are we found. There we are lifted onto the shoulders of the Great Shepherd and carried home to the party of the ages.

Going Deeper

Some days you are one of the ninety-nine, partying at the Shepherd's house. On other days you are the lost one bleating frantically to be found. Either way you have a responsibility. As one of the ninety-nine it is to rejoice when a lost one is found. As a lost one your responsibility is to keep watching for the Shepherd because He is coming for you.

+ Have you ever been one of the "ones" who didn't care about disrupting the status quo or being publicly humiliated because you just needed Jesus so much? What happened?

+ Perhaps you have followed Christ for years, and it's been a long time since you felt like a lost one. What is something you can do today to come alongside Jesus as He hunts for His lost sheep?

> The Son of Man has come to seek and to save that which was lost.
>
> —Luke 19:10

Father, I remember what it was like to be lost. Fill me with compassion for those who feel that way today so I can be Your ambassador to them today. I want to rejoice with heaven when they find You!

THE COST OF THE CROSS (PART 1)

[Grace] is costly because it cost God the life of his Son: "Ye were bought at a price," and what has cost God much cannot be cheap for us.
—DIETRICH BONHOEFFER

As a kid who grew up in the golden age of 1990s Christian rock, I firmly believe the iconic Jesus-rockers, DC Talk, got it right when they penned their classic "Luv Is a Verb." The word *love* might be classified primarily as a noun according to *Merriam-Webster*, but love is certainly not love without action. It must be demonstrated.

I can remember my first crush like it was yesterday. Even though I was only ten, I convinced myself a certain girl was "the one"! However, one gigantic hindrance stood in the way of our potential love connection—my debilitating fear of being rejected. Because of it I never told her my true feelings. I was nervous that she would find out and scorn my love, so I actually treated her worse than other girls. It won't come as a shock to you that nothing ever happened between us, and my ten-year-old heart was irreparably broken (for at least two days). I was a victim of my own inaction. Though the feelings I experienced were strong, because they remained unexpressed, nothing came of our relationship.

Repressed affection is something everyone can relate to, not just insecure ten-year-olds—everyone, that is, except God. There has never been a single moment in time when God hasn't been screaming, "I love you!" in some way, shape, or form. God is love, and love is always expressed. God's agape love is never stagnant or inactive. It's always giving itself away. His love is evident in everything He has done since the beginning of time. Even creation expresses His vast affection for us. Before you were His, He was chasing you down every second of every minute of every day to get what He was after—your heart. The most extravagant expression of God's love happened over two thousand years ago on a hill called Golgotha. To rightly comprehend His love, we have to recognize the gravity of Jesus' obedience at Calvary.

> Greater love has no one than this, that one lay down his life for his friends.
>
> —JOHN 15:13

The Cost of the Cross

Humiliation

Never has a king suffered a more humiliating death than King Jesus. The cross was a greater shame than any human king would ever endure for his people. It's unthinkable that the sovereign King of kings, the Creator of the universe, would choose to die in such an embarrassing way. Marred beyond recognition, spat upon, lied about, abandoned by His disciples, stripped naked, mocked, and scoffed at—Jesus took on all this shame so He could take away ours.

Physical suffering

Having large tracts of flesh peeled back from thirty-nine blows of a cat-o'-nine-tails would have been enough to kill many prisoners in Roman times, but this was only the beginning of Jesus' physical suffering. Many scholars believe the crown of thorns pressed down on Jesus' scalp and skull caused His head to swell to twice its regular size.[1] He carried the instrument of His death up a grueling hill while it dug into His open wounds from the scourging. We can't forget the actual crucifixion, during which giant spikes were driven through Jesus' wrists and feet, each blow more painful than the last. After soldiers hoisted the cross into the air, our Savior had to lift Himself using the nails buried deep in His feet as leverage, enduring excruciating pain, to get a single breath of oxygen in an attempt to relieve His lungs burning from asphyxiation.

Just one of those elements alone is enough to cause me to fall to my knees, overwhelmed at the depth of God's love. Still, this was not the deepest of Christ's sufferings at the cross. The final two areas of His sacrifice were the costliest.

Scorned love

One of the greatest pains anyone can experience is loving vulnerably without receiving love in return. Sincerely and profoundly loving someone without real reciprocation is more excruciating than any physical pain. While Jesus hung on the cross, He had to watch the very ones for whom He was demonstrating His love reject it before His eyes. It was as if the cries of "I love you" that burst forth from His body with every drop of blood fell silent on the dirt of human apathy, lying dormant until the appointed time.

Becoming sin

"[God] made Him who knew no sin to be sin on our behalf, so that we might become the righteousness of God in Him" (2 Cor. 5:21). When I sin against God, the weight of it often feels suffocating before I run to the Father in repentance. I cannot fathom what it must have felt like as Jesus physically took on every sin from every person who ever lived. When we feel the wages of our sin, it's because we've done something wrong. But Jesus had never felt the crushing effects of sin before the cross because He was sinless. But on the cross, even though He knew no sin, He bore the full weight of every sin of every person who has ever lived. He let the weight of sin crush Him so it wouldn't crush us. This crushing caused what I believe to be the most difficult sacrifice of all: "My God, My God, why have You forsaken Me?" (Matt. 27:46).

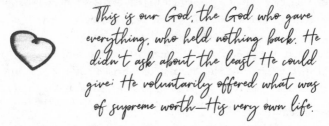

This is our God, the God who gave everything, who held nothing back. He didn't ask about the least He could give; He voluntarily offered what was of supreme worth—His very own life.

This tortured cry, uttered by the Son of God while gasping for His final breaths on the cross, was possibly the only instance in all of the Gospels in which Jesus didn't refer to God as "Father." The consequence of Jesus becoming sin on the cross for us was the Father turning His back on Him. For a moment in time Jesus sacrificed His relationship with the Father so we could forever have the quality of relationship They had always shared. It was the highest expression of love that Jesus and the Father ever demonstrated. They both experienced separation so we would never know separation from them. The pain of this moment is incomprehensible to us because we have never experienced the Father turning His back on us. Jesus took on our sin and volunteered Himself to be separated from the Father so we would never have to experience that kind of pain.

The Father has locked His eyes on us eternally. Even when we fall for the millionth time, He'll never look away. He's overcome with love for us. He's waiting to pour His delight and favor on us constantly.

This is our God, the God who gave everything, who held nothing back. He didn't ask about the least He could give;

He voluntarily offered what was of supreme worth—His very own life. Why? Because He's knocked out about us. To Him the pain of His creation being far from Him was greater than the pain of crucifixion. He would rather let sin crush Him so we could experience freedom. He'd rather bear the cross than bear the thought of us not being together. O, the overwhelming, never-ending, reckless love of God.

Going Deeper

After you have heard the crucifixion story a few times, it is easy to forget what Jesus really went through out of love for us.

- As you read about the crucifixion today, what affected you this time? Express your gratefulness to Christ right now through personal words of worship or a song.

- Can you accept the fact that the joy of having you in His flock kept Jesus on the cross when He had the power to come down? Here's proof:

> Jesus, the author and perfecter of faith...for the joy set before Him endured the cross, despising the shame, and...sat down at the right hand of the throne of God.
> —HEBREWS 12:2

> *Father, it's easy for me to take for granted what Jesus went through for me and for all His lost sheep. The next time I take communion, help me remember this day when I prayerfully recalled what Jesus suffered so I wouldn't have to be separated from You forever. As I take the bread and drink the juice, remind me of this moment and receive it as worship.*

THE COST OF THE CROSS (PART 2)

The reason salvation is so easy to obtain is that it cost God so much.
The Cross was the place where God and sinful man merged with a
tremendous collision and where the way to life was opened. But all
the cost and pain of the collision was absorbed by the heart of God.
—OSWALD CHAMBERS

HAVE YOU EVER participated in a white elephant gift exchange in which everyone is supposed to exchange either inexpensive gifts or pre-owned items that are of no use or value to their owners? There's always that one person who brings something so extravagant and valuable that everyone else at the party leaves feeling shameful at their miserable inadequacy.

I once attended a Valentine's Day party at which I received a gift from a girl whom I had just started dating. Sounds like a sweet moment, right? There was only one problem: I didn't get her anything. Yeah, I know I'm an idiot. Girls love gifts. Period. You could've cut the tension in the room with a knife when I informed her that I hadn't brought her anything because I didn't think our relationship was serious enough for gift-giving. As might be expected, it wasn't long before she decided our relationship wasn't serious enough for continuing at all. Years later the awkwardness and discomfort of that memory still cause me to laugh.

When we look at the staggering gift Jesus gave at the cross, it should cause us to feel woefully unworthy. There's nothing we could give Him in return that would be commensurate. And there's certainly no chance we could hold our own at the divine gift exchange. While I'm obviously not able to endure the spiritual weight of bearing the world's sin (let alone the physical torment), there is something I can offer that's of value to the suffering King—my all. In fact "the joy set before Him" (Heb. 12:2) that we talked about yesterday is all He ever wanted.

This is precisely what Mary of Bethany brought to Jesus just days before He went to the cross—her everything.

> A woman came with a jar of perfume. She had given much money for this. As Jesus ate, she poured the perfume on His head. When the followers saw it, they were angry. They said, "Why was this wasted? This perfume could have been sold for much money and given to poor people."
>
> Jesus knew what they were saying. He said to them, "Why are you giving this woman trouble? She has done a good thing to Me. You will have poor people with you all the time. But you will not have Me with you all the time. She put this perfume on My body to make it ready for the grave. For sure, I tell you, wherever this Good News is preached in all the world, this woman will be remembered for what she has done."
>
> —Matthew 26:7–13, nlv

Jesus had recently disclosed to the disciples that in the coming days He would suffer and die. Instead of bowing in reverent worship at the revelation, the Twelve responded to Jesus' words by debating the theological implications.

However, Mary, whose life had been transformed by sitting at Jesus' feet, chose a different response. Her approach was to find her most expensive possession, a vial of ridiculously costly oil, and pour it out on the feet of the One who gave her life value in the first place. Jesus responded to Mary's sacrifice by declaring that wherever the gospel is preached, what she did would be a memorial. What did Jesus mean by this? He was saying Mary's deed wasn't just a typical knee-jerk reaction to the cross; it was the only appropriate response—everything poured out before the One who poured His life and blood out for us.

Mary's anointing of Jesus is a beautiful foreshadowing of what Jesus was about to do at Calvary. When Christ saw that we were bound in sin, unable to receive the love of the Father, He didn't go shopping at the bargain bin for the cheapest thing He could find to fix the problem. He didn't ask Himself how He could clean up the mess without leaving the safety and comfort of His throne in heaven. No, like Mary, Jesus found the thing which held supreme worth and broke it without regard for the physical and emotional consequences. He smashed the alabaster jar of His life at the cross, and the fragrance of that offering is still drawing sons and daughters to the Father today.

I believe one of the reasons the cross is so overwhelming to us is that we know we could never give back to Jesus a gift that matched all He endured for us. However, just because we can't offer Him something equal to the cross doesn't mean God doesn't require anything from us. He most certainly does! Remember our definition of *love* from yesterday's reading? *Love* is a verb. It demands action. Fortunately we don't have to offer that action in our own strength. The appropriate response to the cross is nothing less than complete and total surrender, by the grace of God.

A good Father never demands something from His

children that they can't give. God never looks at us in our failure and thinks, "Jesus died on the cross, and that was your best effort? What an absolute joke!" That's shame's narrative, not the Father's. Shame tells us our best efforts are never good enough. Shame is a liar, but it is right about one thing: our works pale in comparison with what Jesus did. But here's the good news: the Father isn't asking for equal effort; He's asking for equal surrender. Since offering our entire lives is the only gift worthy of the crucified Savior, He doesn't even consider our works until we first bring Him our hearts. The truth of the grace of the cross should liberate us! We don't have to show up to the gift exchange empty-handed. What love is asking for, we each have in our cupboards.

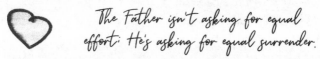

The Father isn't asking for equal effort; He's asking for equal surrender.

I'm not perfect. Many times I've tried my best and come up painfully short. But the cross doesn't shame me for my failure. It doesn't force me to get my act together before I can receive God's goodness. It just kindly asks that when I come, I bring everything I can muster at that moment—and honestly sometimes it isn't much. The cross invites me to bring my all, weak and broken as it may be. It's the exchange the Father has been after the whole time: His heart for mine, His breath of grace for my exhale of effort, His beauty for my ashes.

Going Deeper

What then is the proper response to the overwhelming gift of the cross? Simple. Come to the gift exchange with nothing but your heart—not your pretense, your best efforts, your strengths, or your gifts. All you need to bring is your heart wide open, surrendered, and laid bare before Him.

+ How does Mary's response of pouring out onto Jesus such an expensive treasure challenge you? If you were to "pour out" onto Jesus your most valuable treasure, what would it be? What would it take for you to be able to remove that treasure from your heart and give it to Jesus right now?

+ Consider the following words of the old hymn "When I Survey the Wondrous Cross," and write what they mean to you.

> Were the whole realm of nature mine
> That were an offering far too small
> Love so amazing so divine
> Demands my soul my life my all.[1]

Lord, I feel almost speechless in response to Your sacrifice on the cross. I could never give a gift of that value back to You. But I do give what You ask—all of me. I give myself to the best of my ability and knowledge right now. I look forward to tomorrow, when I will be able to give even more.

LOVING WITH RECKLESS ABANDON

Fearless love looks like this: I don't care what you think of
me; there is a God in heaven who loves you so much that
you won't care who I am by the time you meet Him.
—SHAWN BOLZ

W HEN I WAS a little boy growing up in South Florida, we lived in a townhouse that bordered a major road with heavy traffic just beyond our driveway. My parents were always wary of me playing out front since careless drivers were a legitimate threat to children who didn't understand the seriousness of the situation. I was only allowed to play in front under strict supervision. But that all changed after an incident took place just down the road from us.

One afternoon a young girl was playing with her ball in her front yard when it rolled into the street. The little girl thoughtlessly darted to the road to retrieve her beloved bouncy ball. Her mother, who was sitting on the front porch, looked up just as her daughter got to the edge of the street. Immediately she took off frantically running after her daughter, and without thinking, threw her body in front of the child, acting as a human shield to protect her from oncoming traffic. Fortunately for them both, the driver who struck them was able to slam on the brakes and slow down considerably before impact, so the mother sustained only minor injuries while the daughter escaped the whole thing without so much as a scratch. I wasn't allowed to play in my front yard anymore after that. And we soon found a new house in a quieter, more insulated neighborhood.

What's the moral of the story? Is it that traffic is dangerous? Or maybe that parents these days are too lax? Certainly not! The big takeaway here is that a mother loved her little girl so much that she was willing to put her own life in jeopardy to save her. That is real love. That is real devotion. Real love sacrifices. Real devotion doesn't question the cost. It doesn't consider the consequences; it simply acts when the need arises. Does it know the price might be everything? Yes, but love acts nonetheless.

Just for fun while writing this, I did a quick Google search for something generic like "mom saves child" and found myself inundated with stories of parents going to insane lengths to rescue their kids from danger. I found headlines along the lines of "Cougar-Fighting Mom Saves Son and Lives to Tell About It," "Mother Dies Saving Four Children From Drowning," and "Mom Fights Off Two Men Trying to Snatch Her Baby in Parking Lot." It seems unthinkable, but ludicrous headlines like these are just a click away—*and they're real.*

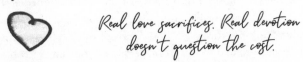

Real love sacrifices. Real devotion doesn't question the cost.

Now imagine headlines such as "Pregnant Mother Protects Homeless Guy From Man-Eating Wolves" or "Mother of Six Staves Off Giant Bloodthirsty Tiger Shark From Attacking Strangers at California Beach." Hard to fathom, right? Altruistic stories like these are hard to come by (perhaps because they don't exist). My point is, most people only make sacrifices such as these when their closest, most dearly beloved blood relatives are in danger. (And even then some of us wouldn't lift a finger!)

But God stepped up to the plate for His kids even while we hated Him. What manner of love is this!

When I first released "Reckless Love," I was overwhelmed with questions concerning the meaning of the song. Because my heart was to pastor people into understanding while minimizing confusion, I penned the following words:

> When I use the phrase "reckless love of God," I'm not saying that God is reckless (careless). I am, however, saying that the way He loves is, in many regards, quite so. What I mean is this: He is utterly unconcerned with the consequences of His actions with regards to His own safety, comfort, and well-being. His love bankrupted heaven for us. His love doesn't consider Himself first. His love isn't selfish or self-serving. He doesn't wonder what He'll gain or lose by giving Himself away. His love isn't cautious. No, it's a love that sent His own Son to die a gruesome death on a cross. The recklessness of His love is seen most explicitly in this—it gets Him hurt over and over. Make no mistake, our sins pain His heart. And "seventy times seven" is a lot of times to get hurt. Yet He opens up and allows us in again and again. His love saw us when we hated Him. When our human depravity caused Him to question whether we'd reject His love, He said, "I don't care. I'm laying My heart on the line, even if it kills Me."

That is the way God loves us. Thoroughly. Completely. Exhaustively. And with utter contempt for what it might cost Him. Many would call this kind of love foolish, even insane, and I'd probably agree with them. When I consider how incredibly jacked up I am, how many character flaws and shortcomings I have, this kind of love doesn't add up. It's quite ridiculous. The apostle Paul in 1 Corinthians 1:18 calls the word of the cross "foolishness." Can't argue with the apostle who wrote half the New Testament, right?

The truth is, despite Jesus' constant, crazy displays of love, we keep chasing our stupid little bouncy balls of sin headlong into traffic day after day. But God, being the good Father He is, keeps running after us despite our foolishness. Using His body as a human shield, He halts speeding vehicles in their tracks, preventing them from crushing us on our journey to maturity. Does it make any sense? Nope. But it sure does move my heart like nothing else. His love gives me value. His sacrifice gives me worth. And it gives you worth too. If He paid for you with His very blood, perhaps you are worth more than you may have once imagined. Give in to this reality. Let it change your paradigms. Let it open your heart. You are deeply loved.

Going Deeper

They say that the value of something is based on what someone else is willing to pay for it. God could not have paid more for you than the price of His own Son, so you are price-less to God. Yet despite your great value, you—and all of us— are called to humble ourselves and serve others. Because Jesus knew His value to God, He was able to serve in the lowest capacity at the last supper.

> Jesus, knowing that the Father had given all things into His hands, and that He had come forth from God and was going back to God, got up from supper, and laid aside His garments; and taking a towel, He girded

Himself. Then He poured water into the basin, and began to wash the disciples' feet.

—John 13:3–5

+ What does this Scripture say about the value Jesus knew He had with God?

+ Jesus knew His identity in God and His value to God. How did this help Him to serve others?

Father, I want to freely serve as Jesus did. I know that He could surrender Himself completely because He knew His place in You, the value You placed on Him. Help me, Lord, to accept Your love and the value You give me so I can be so secure in my identity with You that I can serve others willingly.

NO SHADOW, NO MOUNTAIN

There is no problem too big for God to solve. There is no disease God cannot heal. There is no heart God cannot mend. There is no relationship God cannot restore. There is no sin God cannot redeem. There is no bondage God cannot break. There is no need God cannot meet. There is no mountain God cannot move.
—CHRISTINE CAINE

Humans love stories. Whether it's a toddler nestled in a parent's lap enjoying a picture book or a family gathered around a campfire listening to Granddad talk about the good ol' days, there's just something about story that resonates deeply in the human spirit. Recently I've fallen in love with movies again. Nothing captures my mind and stirs my emotions quite like the silver screen. Some of my favorite flicks contain an epic rescue mission: *Saving Private Ryan*, *Black Hawk Down*, *Jaws* (OK, maybe not *Jaws*). All of these beloved classics keep me on the edge of my seat, drawing me in until I'm practically part of the team on the fateful quest to bring the fallen hero back home.

Two key ingredients in rescue movies bring on the waterworks for me: the valiance and sacrifice of the ones risking their lives and the overwhelming gratefulness in the hearts of those rescued. Many a tear has been shed watching depictions of the recently liberated embrace friends and family after having conceded to the grim reality that they might never see each other again. Meanwhile the heroes of the mission stand proudly in the distance, big beaming smiles on their faces as they witness the reunions and tears of joy bought with their selflessness.

I think these stories pull my heartstrings because they reflect the heart of the gospel. The greatest, most epic rescue mission ever took place two thousand years ago when Jesus became a man to seek and save the lost. The entirety of the incarnation was one massive feat of deliverance. The Father saw us trapped in the snare of sin and death and sent His Son to pay the ultimate price to kick down every prison wall and loosen every chain of bondage that held us captive.

There's truly nothing He won't do to rescue you. When you're in distress, He'll go to the lowest, darkest, and farthest place to bring you home. He'll even leave the ninety-nine to find the one lost sheep. There is, however, one thing that He will not do on His divine rescue mission. He will not take something that is not offered to Him freely. He'll give anything and everything, but He will not forcibly take anything. Why? Because His love is meek.

Jesus' humility sets Him apart from every other ruler in history. All other kings of old had one thing in common: they used their power to take what was not theirs. Our King is different. He never uses power to steal what's not His or force us into anything. His kingly conquest doesn't have coerced submission as its goal, but He desires hearts freely given, won over by His great love. Is He strong enough to take whatever He wants? Absolutely. Yet He exercises restraint in His strength, patiently waiting until we invite Him in. Why? Because He's a God of love, and love always gives the supreme honor of choice. Love without choice is not love at all. In fact there's a word for that kind of thing, and it isn't a pleasant one.

However, some mistake Christ's meekness for impotence,

and in their pride they sabotage their own rescue effort. They get in the way by trying to save themselves. Because they doubt His power and desire to act on their own behalf, they try to bring about spiritual transformation through their own effort and determination.

Practically, we all do this by not coming to God in repentance when we sin. We do this by not crying out for help when we need it. And we do this by not inviting Him into our battles when we desperately need an ally, opting to go it alone instead. Therefore, rather than allowing God to plant us high upon a rock with a new song in our mouths, we get stuck down in the mess we've created, cursing both the story and the author.

When we try to save ourselves, we think we're positioning ourselves to receive God's love, but we're actually resisting it. We believe we are qualifying ourselves for grace, but we're actually disqualifying ourselves. What we need to do is to let ourselves be rescued. If we accept that we are the damsel in distress, powerless to save ourselves, we can climb into the lifeboat of grace Jesus offers us.

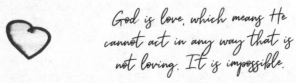

God is love, which means He cannot act in any way that is not loving. It is impossible.

But it is hard for many of us to receive unmerited saving grace. The unworthiness we feel can be overwhelming. Peter experienced this very thing at Passover dinner when Jesus grabbed a bucket and a rag and commenced washing the disciples' feet one by one. I imagine Peter was squirming in his seat as he watched Jesus perform a duty typically relegated to lowly servants. So, when it was Peter's turn to sit in the hot seat (or maybe more appropriately, the cold seat), the oft-brash disciple yelled with pseudo-godly pride, "You shall never wash my feet" (John 13:8, NIV).

Peter probably thought that Jesus was going to be impressed, even honored, by His refusal. I imagine Peter thinking that Jesus would say something like, "Excellent, Peter! I created this entire scenario to see if anyone would recognize the injustice, to see if anyone would realize that I, the greatest of you all, should never perform such a gross and undermining task. You, Peter, have passed the test!" I'm sure ol' Petey was quite shocked when Jesus responded with, "Unless I wash you, you have no part with me" (John 13:8, NIV). The great teacher used an ancient household chore to make a profound and life-changing point: to partake in Jesus' goodness, you must allow yourself to be washed.

Until we let Jesus meet us right in the midst of our failure and filth, He will not save us. God is love, which means He cannot act in any way that is not loving. It is impossible. Taking our hearts without our first offering them is not love; it's theft. The part we get to play in His saving grace is merely allowing Him to do all the forgiving, cleansing, and restoration. He wants to give Himself away. He's already gone to insane lengths to find us and provide a way back home; all we have to do is acquiesce to the collision of grace on the prodigal road.

Going Deeper

Imagine Jesus walking into your home right now while you're just sitting in your living room.

+ **What do you picture Him doing? What do you picture Him saying?**

If you're like me, your mind will go right to how embarrassed you are about everything that's out of place. You are suddenly laser-focused on the dirty dishes in the sink, the shoes left in the middle of the floor, or even worse, the music or movies lying around that might not meet with His approval.

Here's what the story of the foot washing teaches us: if you can't imagine Jesus walking into your mess with a massive smile on His face or if you can't see Him walking straight into the kitchen and doing your dishes without shaming you, you probably don't have the right picture of Jesus. When the rescue boat of His love finds you drowning in your failure, you can't try to save yourself. You must overcome pride and allow Him to pull you aboard.

> He who did not spare his own Son, but gave him up for us all—how will he not also, along with him, graciously give us all things?
>
> —ROMANS 8:32, NIV

Father, I choose now to receive all the love You have for me. If You gave up Your Son, You will surely give me everything else I need. I freely offer all to You. I want to be meek like Jesus and pleasing to You, as He was. I receive Your grace, all of it—your undeserved, unearned grace—and I respond with joy and thankfulness.

WHILE WE WERE YET SINNERS

[God] has a single relentless stance toward us: He loves us. He
is the only God man has ever heard of who loves sinners.
—Brennan Manning

Sometimes in the theatre of my mind, I like to imagine
bizarre things—not creepy things, just really weird
things. I know, I know, I'm a very odd person. Nevertheless,
in one of my recent offbeat fantasies, I imagined how mortal
enemies might react if forced to show affection to one another.
A kiss, an embrace, a kind word—you know, just a little love.
Can you imagine Luke Skywalker hugging it out with Emperor
Palpatine? How about Frodo Baggins laying his head on Sau-
ron's breast? Thor planting a big wet one on Thanos' cheek? Not
weird enough for you? How about John Wick inviting the gang-
sters who killed his puppy over for midday tea and crumpets?

Well, I was having a good chuckle at that one when the
ultimate be-all and end-all scenario popped into my mind:
I saw Jesus lovingly holding Satan's hand. My first thought
was to laugh, but then out of nowhere, some dormant, hyper-
religious thing piqued inside of my mind. "NO! Get that filth
out of your head!" it demanded.

Yet the picture was so vivid: Jesus in His sandals and long
white robe next to Satan, an ugly, bloated, red creature with
a tail and pitchfork, the two in a locked gaze. I'll admit that
while it was a hilarious thought at first, I definitely scanned
the room suspiciously, worried that the enormity of my sac-
rilegious daydream might be detected. I could practically feel
people's judgmental stares searing into my soul.

But the oddity of the picture got me thinking. The Bible says in Romans 5:8 that "while we were yet sinners, Christ died for us." Furthermore, in Romans 8:7, it says, "The carnal mind is enmity against God" (NKJV). The word *enmity* indicates having deep-seated hatred or ill will toward someone. So Paul is basically saying while we hated God, He loved us. When we wanted nothing to do with Him, His loved pursued us. Like the lyric of "Reckless Love" says, when we were His foes, still His love fought for us. Even when we warred against Him, kicking and screaming in our iniquity, His love battled for our hearts.

All of a sudden the picture of Jesus holding Satan's hand didn't seem so absurd. Now, I'm not saying that we should be praying for the salvation of the devil or anything, but I am proposing that maybe the fact that He loved us when we hated Him is more like the picture of Jesus and an ugly devil than the image of Jesus and a lovely damsel in distress.

> The revelation of our intrinsic "badness" might seem like something to get depressed about when instead it should be the diving board that launches us into full-on praise and worship.

You might think, "I never hated God. I just wasn't a Christian yet." Many believe people are mostly good from birth, but that idea downplays what the Bible says about unbelievers. Paul used some pretty intense language when referring to them: "Do not be unequally yoked with unbelievers. For what partnership has righteousness with lawlessness? Or what fellowship has light with darkness?" (2 Cor. 6:14, ESV). Unbelievers are called lawless and dark, not pre-saved and full of light. This goes against the belief that man is inherently good.

But didn't God declare all that He had made, including Adam, to be "very good" in the garden (Gen. 1:31)? Yes, He did, but that was before the fall of man (and woman). Romans 5 tells us that sin came into the world through one man (Adam) and spread to all so that by one man's disobedience all became sinners (v. 12). If you're anything like me, you're thinking, "That's not fair!" And you're right—it's not. But it is true. The reality is, God still wanted us even when we were steeped in sin, running away from Him as fast as we could.

The revelation of our intrinsic "badness" might seem like something to get depressed about when instead it should be the diving board that launches us into full-on praise and worship. When we realize how far gone we were and how grim our diagnosis was, the love of God makes sense. We were hopeless cases, diagnosed with the most aggressive of cancers—sin—but God, the great physician, saw something in us that caused Him to sacrifice everything for the cure. His life for ours. It's like a doctor giving his life for a random patient—and not only that, a patient who cursed him and treated him with utter contempt, refusing his help and threatening to run out. No doctor in his right mind would do this. We must realize that each of us was once that patient. If we think we were healthy and awesome before God found us, we will never appreciate the gravity of His sacrifice to heal us. But when we see the lengths to which He went, everything comes into perspective; everything makes sense.

So next time you think you've got the love of God figured out, next time you're bored by the cross of Christ, meditate on Romans 5:6–8 (MSG): "Christ arrives right on time to make this happen. He didn't, and doesn't, wait for us to get ready. He presented himself for this sacrificial death when we were far too weak and rebellious to do anything to get ourselves ready. And even if we hadn't been so weak, we wouldn't have known what to do anyway. We can understand someone dying for a person worth dying for, and we can understand how someone good and noble could inspire us to selfless sacrifice. But God put his love on the line for us by offering his Son in sacrificial death while we were of no use whatever to him."

Because while we were yet sinners, Christ died for us. It wasn't a fair deal; it wasn't an equitable transaction. God gave us His beauty, and we gave Him our ashes. It doesn't make any sense, yet He delights to make the divine exchange. His mercy is not weakness; it triumphs over judgment (Jas. 2:13).

Going Deeper

There's something inside us, probably going back to the tree of the knowledge of good and evil, that wants to earn our own way and not depend on another's mercy or charity. We want to act independently, but the gospel does not allow for that because that puts us in enmity against God.

+ **What comes to mind when you think of being dependent on someone?**

Most of us feel that we grow out of dependence as we become independent. But with God, we never outgrow dependence. Make a list of everything from God that you are dependent on right now.

Convert this list into a hymn of praise to God for all the ways He allows you, in the midst of your desire for self-sufficiency, to depend so fully on Him. Thank Him for every way you must depend on Him, because through these things He is drawing you into deep relationship with Him.

SECTION II

FORGET WHAT YOU THINK YOU KNOW

WHO DO YOU SAY I AM?

What comes into our minds when we think about
God is the most important thing about us.
—A. W. TOZER

ABOUT TEN YEARS ago, I read a book that changed my life. A. W. Tozer's *Knowledge of the Holy* wrecked me in the best way possible. Here's an excerpt that I think encapsulates the heart of the author's message perfectly.

> Let us beware lest we in our pride accept the erroneous notion that idolatry consists only in kneeling before visible objects of adoration, and that civilized peoples are therefore free from it. The essence of idolatry is the entertainment of thoughts about God that are unworthy of him. It begins in the mind and may be present where no overt act of worship has taken place.... Wrong ideas about God are not only the fountain from which the polluted waters of idolatry flow; they are themselves idolatrous. The idolater simply imagines things about God and acts as if they were true.[1]

I remember putting the book down and slumping into my chair as the weight of those words hit me like a Mack truck. I had always laughed at the absurdity of Israel bowing down to false gods crafted by their own hands. I mean, wasn't it so obvious to them that their idols were just cheap counterfeits of the real thing? I considered myself far too pious to stoop to such inanity. But as I pondered Tozer's words, the Holy Spirit spoke to my arrogance. "Your mind is an idol-making factory.

Every day you fashion thoughts about who I am and what I'm like that aren't based in truth, and those wrong thoughts fuel your wrong decisions. You're no less guilty than Israel." Well, color me convicted.

Surprisingly, even though I was being corrected, it didn't feel as if God was angry with me. On the contrary, I felt His immense kindness as He shepherded me to a better path. That "hurts-so-good" moment forever changed the way I thought about God.

Romans 12:2 (NIV) says, "Do not conform to the pattern of this world, but be transformed by the renewing of your mind. Then you will be able to test and approve what God's will is— his good, pleasing and perfect will." When I first read that verse, I figured the way to renew my mind was to try my absolute hardest not to think worldly thoughts. If I could muster enough willpower never to think about sinful things, then I could fulfill Scripture's command. But when I read that Tozer quote, the Father showed me a picture. I was trying to tear down altars built to false gods without replacing them with altars of true worship. It just doesn't work like that. It's like removing weeds without pulling up the roots—they grow right back. We must get to the roots of the lies and replace them with seeds of truth. The key for me wasn't trying harder not to think about the bad stuff but rather renewing my mind by meditating on the good stuff of Scripture, which in turn transformed my image of the Father.

If our minds think rightly about God, our wills and emotions will flourish in the garden of those truths.

Like following a loose thread on a sweater until you find the point at which the unraveling began, tracing every failure in our lives will lead back to a lie about God's nature. For example, I might lash out at someone in anger, but ultimately I can trace that action back to a lie that says God is mean or unkind. I don't tear down that altar just by repenting of the action but by pinpointing the lie that led to that action and repenting of that. Then I ask the Father to tell me what He thinks about me because I know His thoughts are higher than mine and He can't wait to share them with me. Bill Johnson says, "I can't afford to have a thought in my head about me that He doesn't have in His."[2] I can't tear down the strongholds in my own strength, but the Father can demolish even their very framework with just one word from His mouth.

The mind is like a gate. It's the first line of defense for what comes in and what goes out. If our minds think rightly about God, our wills and emotions will flourish in the garden of those truths. The opposite is true as well: if we don't pluck out wrong ideas, our inner man will eventually be choked out. Thinking rightly about the Father is the most important assignment for our minds.

Allow me to illustrate this point using one of my favorite movies, *Inception*. In this film the main character, Dom Cobb, has a rare ability to enter people's dreams to plant or extract thoughts. Dom is hired to enter the subconscious of a man named Fischer, a billionaire business owner with a fractured relationship pivotal to the plot. The plan is to plant an idea so deep in Fischer's head that it would cause him to break up his father's recently inherited business. Cobb knows there's only one idea powerful enough to catalyze such a weighty decision—his perception of his father.

In the narrative of the film Fischer believes his father is disappointed with the person he's become. This disapproval fuels him to keep the business in an attempt to prove everyone wrong by running it better than his father ever had. Therefore Cobb's goal is to remove the idea that Fischer's dad is dissatisfied with him. He knows, however, that he can't simply remove that one isolated thought because Fischer's mind will replace it with another of his father's displeasure. So instead, Cobb decides to plant a new memory into his mind.

In the film's beautiful and moving culmination Cobb takes Fischer back to his father's deathbed. There Fischer expects his father to berate him concerning his failures. But to his surprise his father expresses love and pride over the man he's become. The mission succeeds, and Fischer sells the business because his heart is healed knowing that his father is proud of him.

We humans are like Fischer. We wrongly interpret our memories, and then they become assumptions about the Father's disposition—assumptions that He's disappointed in us or, at the very least, just not very nice. The Holy Spirit is like Cobb. He's on a mission to find every lie about the Father so He can extract them and plant the truth in their place. But He only does this in partnership with us, with our cooperation. This concept is illustrated brilliantly in 2 Corinthians 10:5 (NKJV), where Paul encourages us to cast down "arguments and every high thing that exalts itself against the knowledge of God, bringing every thought into captivity to the obedience of Christ." When we partner with the Holy Spirit, He turns the circumstances we've misinterpreted into portraits on which to vividly emblazon His love and kindness—even amid pain—if we only let Him.

Going Deeper

In C. S. Lewis' famous children's allegory *The Lion, the Witch and the Wardrobe*, Aslan is a lion who represents God. Mr. Beaver describes Aslan to Lucy by saying, "He isn't safe. But he's good."[3] I think Lewis' distinction between God being safe and being good is a lot like my choice to describe God's love as reckless. Reckless seems negative; unsafe seems negative. Yet both descriptions have been ascribed to a good God.

- Do you have a perception of God that you now see is probably inaccurate? What is it? Why is it wrong?

- In my situation I was surprised when God responded with kindness when I realized how I had been entertaining idols. Is there a situation in your life that you need to admit and fully trust to God but have been afraid to because you are afraid of His reaction?

- Think of a situation in your past in which you had to trust in God's goodness, even when things looked bad. How does remembering how God brought you through that uncertain time encourage you to trust God in your current situation?

> [Cast] all your anxiety on Him, because He cares for you.
>
> —1 Peter 5:7

LOSE YOUR RELIGION

The greatest single cause of atheism in the world today
is Christians, who acknowledge Jesus with their lips, then
walk out the door, and deny Him by their lifestyle. That is
what an unbelieving world simply finds unbelievable.
—BRENNAN MANNING

WHEN I WAS a kid (a naughty kid, mind you), I used to lie in bed each night before dozing off and nonchalantly "repent" for all the sins I'd committed that particular day. Honestly each day there were so many I couldn't recount them one by one, so I'd give God a few broad-stroke pleasantries about being "really sorry" and call it a night. My understanding of God was so skewed and erroneous that I had reduced Him to just another bogeyman under my bed at night, a ghost trying to get me if I didn't recite the proper combination of words or wear the right silver crucifix. To me God was just another powerful but mostly malignant entity (not unlike Dracula or Wolfman), poised to devour me as soon as I did something to irk Him. Despite not having a relationship with God, I still had a healthy fear of Him, which compelled me to cover all my bases with a quick, disingenuous prayer before laying my head on my pillow at night.

Christianity was, to me, merely a list of dos and don'ts (mostly don'ts). Around my house, the ethos revolved more around what we couldn't do than what we should do as followers of Christ. We were more concerned with what we weren't than what we were. I knew more about the issues we were against than the issues we were for. The reason I prayed the sinner's prayer every night was because my understanding of religion was basically this: do the right things and you might make it into heaven by the skin of your teeth; but do the wrong things and God will toss you into the fiery pit of hell with great enjoyment and zero remorse.

Around my house, the ethos revolved more around what we couldn't do than what we should do as followers of Christ. We were more concerned with what we weren't than what we were. I knew more about the issues we were against than the issues we were for.

Church was just one of the many boxes to check off, along with other things like trying your best to pray; refraining from cursing, drinking, and smoking; and most boring of all, reading the Bible. As understood through the mind of a twelve-year-old, the mantra of Christianity could have gone something like this:

1. Try not to tick God off, and He might spare you from the eternal torment He was looking forward to banishing you to.

2. If you keep Him happy by doing all the stuff your parents tell you to do, one day you'll get to ride on a cloud, playing a harp in heaven forever.

Wow, sounds like great fun, huh? To me Christianity was more of a religious questionnaire based on behavior than an authentic set of convictions birthed in the place of real relationship with a loving God.

In my mind God was angry all the time. Somewhere along the line I'd read Jonathan Edwards' sermon, "Sinners in the Hands of an Angry God," and, boy, did it take hold in my spirit. Because I didn't have a substantial relationship with God through which I could rightly metabolize Edwards' writings, what should have been an awe-inspiring piece on the power and beauty of a holy God just scared me to death.

I remember attending church on Sundays (and Wednesdays and Fridays and Saturdays for potluck lunch) and being confused during worship as I watched people rapturously sing to this God I knew to be so miserly—all with smiles on their faces to boot! I remember thinking they must have become good at acting so God wouldn't strike them with a bolt of punitive lightning right then and there. From my perspective the ones who enjoyed it the most must have been the worst sinners in the whole place; they had more reason to cover up how they really felt!

It wasn't until the ripe old age of nineteen that I genuinely began to understand the love of God. I was living in Kansas City, taking part in an internship for young adults who wanted to love Jesus. During a teaching on the eternity of God, all of a sudden (although I wasn't even paying attention) the Holy Spirit filled the room in a way I'd never experienced before.

Though I'd grown up in church my whole life, I'd never felt the tangible presence of God in that way. I began weeping violently. Not the quiet, peaceful, one-tear-streaming-down-your-face kind of weeping. I'm talking about the loud, long, snot-filled, embarrassing kind. I remember having zero comprehension of what was transpiring in that moment. Through the tears I was thinking, "What is going on?! What am I feeling?!" That's when God decided to speak.

I heard two things very clearly in my spirit. The first was, "Cory, I've seen everything you've done since you were a little boy." This realization was weighty for me, considering how bad of a young person I was. In my teenage years I'd gotten into drugs, alcohol, and promiscuity, so it was tough to grapple with the gravity of learning that God had seen it all.

I quickly realized that I was feeling the fear of the Lord. Somehow I cried even harder than before, genuinely repenting for my sin, feeling the full weight of the pain I'd caused Him. It wasn't a trite bedtime apology from a twelve-year-old anymore; it was an oh-my-gosh-I've-pained-the-heart-of-a-holy-God kind of "I'm sorry!"

In rapid succession God spoke the second phrase to my heart, "Cory, I still want you, and I still love you." His words wrecked me. Could it be that after all these years of falsely believing God was a tyrant set only on oppressing the good people of the earth, in reality He was a kind Father just waiting for me to come home? Could it be that He had loved me all along, even when I least expected it? I wept for another hour under His tenderness.

Going Deeper

God's kindness toward me wrecked me. I didn't know God, and I didn't know that His disposition toward me—and you—is kindness.

> For we also once were foolish ourselves, disobedient,
> deceived, enslaved to various lusts and pleasures,
> spending our life in malice and envy, hateful, hating
> one another. But when the kindness of God our Savior
> and His love for mankind appeared, He saved us, not
> on the basis of deeds which we have done in righteous-
> ness, but according to His mercy.
>
> —Titus 3:3–5

We have to be careful that we don't try to describe God
with misconceptions that come from our finite minds or our
reactions to circumstances.

+ Have you ever had a significant moment of connection with
  God in which He surprised you with His kindness? What
  happened?

+ How can remembering God's kindness toward you help you
  respond with kindness toward others who don't deserve it
  either?

Day 13

FATHERS, SONS, AND THE HOLY SPIRIT

Your heavenly Father...sees the secret place in your heart that cries out for the unconditional love of a father, for the affirmation and affection that only He can provide. His compassion and mercy are available to you...He wants you in His loving embrace!
—JACK FROST

PEOPLE WHO KNOW anything about me know that I am one of the most competitive humans on the planet. I love playing sports. There's just something spiritual about getting out with a bunch of dudes and leaving it all on the field (or the court or the rink—whatever floats your boat). The release of aggression and stress I get from athletics is almost euphoric. Plus I love to win.

As I write this, I'm remembering last night at my local gym when I was playing a few games of basketball with some songwriting friends who were in town. All was going well. (I was dominating as usual.) Our team was down by a few points, and we needed a boost, so I started going harder and harder to the rack. (For those of you who don't know basketball lingo, this means dribbling the ball to the basket with force.) Then the unexpected happened: I sprained my ankle. I went up strong for a layup after a hard drive and landed on someone's foot. The three pops from my lower leg were audible (and nauseating) even in a loud, reverberant gym. As I'm writing this, my leg is propped up and nearly frozen from the ice packs I've been applying every ten minutes. Thankfully the post-sprain events were redemptive, and dare I say, even God ordained.

As I lay there writhing in pain, screaming words that

probably should never come out of a believer's mouth, all the guys in the gym (Christian and non-Christian) gathered around me to pray. While I couldn't appreciate it at the time due to the excruciating agony, in retrospect it was a touching scene. Afterward they found some ice and carried me to a couch where a heartfelt conversation broke out.

A couple of the guys recognized that I was "the 'Reckless Love' guy" (as many people know me now) and began to ask questions about the story behind the song. I shared that when I was growing up, my dad was a harsh man who often spoke abusively to my sister and me. It wasn't until I had my first son that I began to understand the love of God. I explained to them that our earthly fathers often shape our view of the heavenly Father.

As I spoke, two of the young men were visibly touched, with tears and snot flowing copiously. I could tell the Father was up to something. As the ten of us gathered around my swelling ankle, it was as if these two had found a safe space to unload their burdens and the gym had transformed from a court to a cathedral.

The first to speak, a young black man from Chicago, opened up about how his dad wasn't around at all growing up. To make matters more complicated, he had just found out that the man he believed to be his uncle all of his life was more than likely his biological father. He cried as he confessed that all of it made him feel unwanted, unloved, and unfit to start a family of his own.

The second to pipe up, a young Hispanic kid from Detroit, had just been released from jail after a two-year stint. He told us about his daughter and how he only got to see her twice a week and every other weekend. It visibly hurt him to tell us that because he didn't want his little girl to think of him in the same way he thought of his dad—as mostly absent and unavailable. He wanted to break the cycle of neglect and abandonment but didn't know how.

It's funny that even as grown men and women, our earthly fathers dramatically affect our views of life and God. They still play a vital role in our understanding of the things around us, even if we don't want them to or if we think we've shut them out of our lives completely. Sometimes we think we can rise above their shortcomings in a pull-yourself-up-by-your-bootstraps kind of mentality, but when we honestly dive into the deep places of our hearts, we discover that the wounds inflicted by our father figures still shape the way we see the world.

It's not until we find healing from the wounds that our viewpoints can change. Until we rectify the original image, we will continue to see God and the world as cruel and out to get us. And the only way we rectify the original image is by going back to the source—our very first snapshot(s) of God. We must allow the Father to take us back to the beginning and change the narrative from calloused to kind, from guilty to good. In this place of vulnerability He can rewrite the story of our lives.

There are no perfect fathers; even the best of them can only point to the one true, perfect Father. Whether your dad was good, bad, or indifferent (or maybe even nonexistent), he will fall short of the good Father in whose image we were all made. Without a doubt every one of us will end up with a few scars and wounds along the way; that's just the price we pay for real love. When we choose to love deeply, we risk getting hurt greatly. But the Lord in His wisdom allows what He could easily prevent in His power. Don't ask God why; instead ask Him what you can give Him through the pain, confusion, or difficulty that you couldn't give in another situation.

Even though I don't subscribe to the theology that God causes bad things to happen to us, last night I found myself believing that God had allowed my injury so I'd sit down and have a conversation with those guys. I guess in the bigger picture of things, my injured ligaments were a small and temporal sacrifice for a moment that would last a lifetime (and who knows—maybe ten lifetimes).

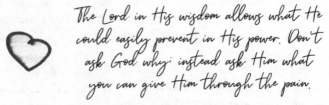

The Lord in His wisdom allows what He could easily prevent in His power. Don't ask God why; instead ask Him what you can give Him through the pain.

We cried together, shared stories, and became the church together. We vowed to let God into the deepest, darkest places of our souls. We promised that the work God had begun in the gym wouldn't end there, but that we'd take the healing to our homes and from there to the streets because God knows there are a lot of people with jacked-up images of the Father out there. I know because I was one of them. The truth is, He's just waiting—or better yet, bursting with wild anticipation—for the chance to step in and crush any lies about the reality of who He is.

Going Deeper

Today will you invite God into any corridors of your soul that have been walled off for years or maybe even decades? Will you be honest with Him about the things that hurt you, disappointed you, and broke you—even if it involves your father or God Himself? It's OK. God is good and kind. He won't leave your questions unanswered. He won't keep you in the dark. There's no shadow He won't light up. There's no wall He won't kick down. And just one word from God's mouth can shatter a thousand lies.

* Choose one hurtful or disappointing thing that came to mind just now. Picture God just sitting across from you in a casual setting. Start talking to Him about it, pausing at times to listen to Him.

* How has your perception of God changed as a result of this time? Explain.

> The LORD is good to all; he has compassion on all he has made.
>
> —PSALM 145:9, NIV

LEARNING TO BE SONS AND DAUGHTERS

We never know the love of a parent till we become parents ourselves.
—HENRY WARD BEECHER

Y WIFE AND I married young. Anna was twenty, and I was twenty-one. We were just kids, but, boy, were we in love. Before we even started dating, we were best friends for almost a year. No one could separate us. I lived to make her laugh, and she genuinely found me funny. It was a match made in heaven.

But when we officially became boyfriend and girlfriend, everything changed. My confident, funny air of youthful assurance suddenly vanished, only to be replaced by the soft-spoken, awkward insecurity of a little boy. I'm not sure exactly how it happened, but it was terrible.

Our first real date was at Chipotle (fancy, right?), and I hardly said a word the whole time. I just sat there, timid and unsure of myself. Let me tell you, she wasn't laughing anymore. I knew I was doomed. She called the next day to tell me she was breaking up with me. I cried uncontrollably for a week straight and then finally found the courage to ask her to give me another chance. This scenario repeated itself three more times during our dating relationship. It was the weirdest thing, but when push came to shove, I didn't know how to be a man. I couldn't muster the strength to stand confident and resolute in a relationship that might affect the rest of my life.

Fast forward about three years. Anna and I were expecting our first child—a son. We were so insanely pumped up (and simultaneously freaked out). It was all we could think about.

Still, I remember feeling a lot of anxiety related to raising him. If you'll recall what I wrote in yesterday's devotion, I dealt with some traumatic stuff as a kid, and I was terrified I'd have some of the same propensities my dad did. Growing up around verbal abuse can take a toll on a person's psyche, and I was definitely feeling its effects. In fact, during this time of my life, I was struggling to grasp the love of God and—probably more accurately and honestly—God in general.

It felt as if my sinful proclivities and obvious shortcomings were always right in front of my face. Sometimes they were all I could see. I viewed my entire existence through the lens of my failure, and I could always hear my dad's voice in the back of my head telling me I wasn't good enough and that no matter how hard I tried, I'd still be too weak, too small, or too stupid.

The first year or two of our marriage had been hard. I was beginning to realize I was a very arrogant person (this came as no surprise to anyone but me). I thought I knew everything. I thought everyone else was wrong but never considered that I might be the misguided one. This mindset did not go over well in a new marriage (to put it lightly).

To make matters worse, Anna and I had been living on about $1000 per month and barely had enough money to pay our mortgage and eat, let alone furnish our first (1100-square-foot) house and do the things most newlyweds enjoy. As the birth of our first child drew near, it was as if the whole world was caving in around me, and the words that continuously echoed in my mind were, "You're not good enough."

Gabriel Phinehas Asbury was born November 6, 2009, after more than twenty-four hours of labor. (Yes, you read that correctly. My wife is a champ!) Our baby boy was finally here, and to this day I vividly remember the first time I held him. It was as if time stood still and the rest of the world melted away. (It could've been because I hadn't slept in more than thirty hours, but who knows?) I stared into his dark eyes and marveled at his raven black head of hair. It was only him and me in a locked gaze, and I wasn't going anywhere. Now, I can't lie to you. He looked kind of like a little alien as most newborns do, but that didn't change the way I felt about him.

At that moment, a capacity for love that I didn't know existed opened up inside of me. It's like my heart grew ten sizes in a matter of ten seconds. You know that scene in *The Grinch* when his half-dead heart turns bright red and swells enormously inside of him? It felt like that times a million.

At that moment, I realized a couple of things. First I knew there was nothing Gabriel could do to make me love him less. No evil deed, no temper tantrum, no crime he could commit could change the way I felt about him. Conversely, nothing he could do would make me love him more. He could say all the right words, draw the right picture, grow up to receive the right scholarship, and get the right job—but nothing could cause me to love him any more than I did right there at that moment. And the beauty of the whole thing was, he literally couldn't do anything for me at that time. All he could do was cry and poop and poop and cry—that's it.

He's a Father who adores His children right where they are. His love isn't based on what we can do or produce for Him; it's based on who we are—His sons and daughters.

In that hospital room (actually it was a birthing center hallway because we didn't have enough money to go to the hospital) I had an epiphany, probably the most important realization of my life thus far. God thinks about me the same way I think about Gabriel—He's completely, thoroughly, ridiculously knocked out about me. There's not a thing I could do to change His mind.

He's a Father who adores us, His children, right where we are. His love isn't based on what we can do or produce for Him; it's based on who we are—His sons and daughters. We are His image bearers. We look like Him. We've got His eyes, His smile, His likeness. In Jesus we are the righteousness of God (2 Cor. 5:21), and He's head over heels about us.

This revelation changed everything for me. I began to see myself this way. As I beheld my son, I saw myself the way I saw him: adored, delighted in, and cherished. The nagging questions in my head concerning my character were answered as I let the Father speak truth and identity over me. The old mantra "You're not good enough" slowly transformed into "You are enough!" Even the old patterns of sin began to change as I let the Father rewrite the story of my life. It was amazing. I had to become a father to learn how to become a son. I had to let go of my arrogance and let God love me into wholeness.

Going Deeper

Are you a father or a mother, an aunt or an uncle? If so, perhaps you've had an experience like mine in which you've understood the Father's love when you held your little one. There's nothing like looking into the eyes of one who reflects back some image of yourself to make the love just pour out of you. And it pours out of the Father for us too.

> See what great love the Father has lavished on us,
> that we should be called children of God! And that
> is what we are!
>
> —1 JOHN 3:1, NIV

Read the scripture above out loud, putting your name in.

♦ **How might your view of yourself be different if you read this
scripture about yourself several times a day for a month?**

♦ **How might your view of God be different if you did that?**

I challenge you to try it. If we keep doing the same thing,
we will keep getting the same results. If you want to receive a
new revelation of God's love for you, try something new!

Day 15

CAN'T EARN IT, DON'T DESERVE IT

God's love isn't based *on me. It's simply* placed *on me.*
—Lysa TerKeurst

How many of us have tried to earn our way into God's good graces, as if His affection were a prize to be won by the biggest and strongest? Like a race of Darwinian proportions, this long and grueling competition called life convinces us that only the fastest and most determined will earn the trophy of God's approval. How many times have we deprived ourselves of joy or pleasure thinking that our ascetic attempts to do more (or less) through self-discipline will earn His love and somehow, in some way, grant us a more favorable position in heaven?

We sing, dance, write, paint, and do anything and everything in a desperate attempt to get Him to look our way. We flail and act out for His attention like a bunch of toddlers with daddy issues screaming, "Look at me! Watch what I can do!" Most of us fail to realize that His eyes have been on us and His heart has been for us from the very minute we were born. Scripture tells us that He formed us in our mother's wombs and cared for us deeply even before we entered the cosmos. Before the foundations of the world we were the dreams of His heart. He never sleeps, He never slumbers, and we're the first thoughts on His mind.

Scripture tells us that God formed us in our mother's wombs and cared for us deeply even before we entered the cosmos. Before the foundations of the world we were the dreams of His heart.

I believe we think we can somehow earn God's love because we've grown up in a world that tells us we have to do something to get something. The consumeristic, capitalistic systems that drive our culture want us to believe we need more and more. They continually feed us the lie that we never have enough. So what do we do? We work our fingers to the bone trying to achieve and acquire—more money, better jobs, more expensive clothes, bigger houses and cars, more exotic vacations, and the latest tech toys—but we're never satisfied, and nothing is ever good enough.

This same mentality seeps right into the church. As Christians we spend our lives striving for unrealistic goals that keep us perpetually running on the hamster wheel of dead religion. We think we're "movin' on up" to bigger and better things, when the truth is, none of our efforts gets us any closer to the real goal.

That's because God's system is not the same as the world's system. Romans 8 tells us, "Therefore, there is now no condemnation for those who are in Christ Jesus, because through Christ Jesus the law of the Spirit who gives life has set you free from the law of sin and death. For what the law was powerless to do because it was weakened by the flesh, God did by sending his own Son in the likeness of sinful flesh to be a sin offering" (vv. 1–3, NIV). Here we see Paul proving an essential and foundational point of New Testament Christianity to the often results-oriented Romans: following the law was never meant to be an indicator of a complete believer because the truth is, no one (or should I say only One) could completely fulfill its tenets. Instead the law was an overt way to show us that we cannot do it on our own and we need a Savior.

I fall into this trap a lot. Like Paul in Philippians 3 I seek to prove my pedigree, citing all the great things I've done for God since I was born. The mindset is "the more I do, the better I am." However, the crux of Paul's teaching in Philippians 3 is that his pedigree wasn't worth a crap (the Greek word is *skybalon*, which the King James translates appropriately as "dung"[1]). Without purity of heart all of our works are like clanging cymbals (1 Cor. 13:1). We must hear the voice of God over our lives before we can do anything significant for Him.

I can hear some of you screaming at me through the pages, "OK, Cory, you've told us *a lot* about the problem. Now give us the key to fix it!" Well, I've got good news and bad news for you. There's a simple remedy, but it's usually not a quick fix.

Like Adam in the garden we must hear the voice of God declaring identity over us before we've done anything to earn it. After all of creation was made, God painted His masterpiece: mankind. He looked at Adam's newly formed body, and He proclaimed over him with pleasure, "This is very good!" He stooped down into the dust of the earth to breathe the breath of life into Adam's lungs, and as Adam opened his eyes with consciousness for the first time, the very first words he hears are those of life-giving identity. I imagine this was a wondrous exchange—the God of the ages kneeling in the dirt of humanity. What an incredible picture!

We also must go back to the beginning, back before life programmed us to do only to get. Here we must listen to the Good Shepherd calling us by name. We must hear Him tell us who we are. Then and only then will we be able to truly walk in our calling and identity as sons and daughters of God.

In the garden we see one of the purest expressions of the relationship between God and man. At the dawn of creation, before sin got in the way, we catch a glimpse into what the Father intended, into what was always the greatest desire of His heart: a walk in the cool of the day with His son. Nothing grand, nothing magnificent—just a slow, unhurried amble through the garden He created for our pleasure. Adam hadn't done a single thing to earn a stroll with God every evening (or morning, depending on which scholar you read), yet without fail, the Father met Him there.

I want to suggest that God did this for one reason alone: He *liked* Adam. He couldn't get enough of him. Adam hadn't built God an altar or a worship sanctuary or a church or anything, for that matter. He hadn't written God a song or painted the Mona Lisa. Adam hadn't plumbed the depths of theological pontification; he hadn't preached a soul-winning sermon. He hadn't brought about world peace. No, Adam simply tended the garden the way he was asked to, knowing that each evening, rest would descend upon the earth and God would step into his reality just to be with him.

Adam had an understanding of God's vast, ridiculous affection for him, and that fueled everything. With that at the forefront of his mind Adam consistently kept beautiful the place where the divine collision occurred: the garden. It was his only job. Adam's work was from delight and delight was from work, just as it was meant to be.

Going Deeper

Guilt, shame, and fear are three compulsions that drive us to try to earn God's love and approval through our actions and accomplishments. Although we have likely experienced all of these, one of them might be predominant in motivating your actions.

+ Did either guilt, shame, or fear resonate with you the most as a motivating force behind some of your actions? What is the first example that pops into your mind?

+ Take a few minutes to ask God where that guilt, shame, or fear came from. What is behind it?

This may be the beginning of the healing of your identity in God. Accept this as a small step toward a fresh identity that matches how God sees you. Ask God to lead you in the next steps you need to take to explore this further and receive your new identity.

> [God] has saved us and called us with a holy calling, not according to our works, but according to His own purpose and grace which was granted us in Christ Jesus from all eternity.
>
> —2 TIMOTHY 1:9

Day 16

OUR GOODNESS DOESN'T CUT IT

God wants to get us off the treadmill of religion and
into beautiful relationship with the Father.
—Jonathan Helser

I N Psalm 16:2 David writes, "My goodness is nothing apart from You" (NKJV). What a cheery scripture to kick off today's reading, right? I can hear some of your thoughts now. "Wow, I have no goodness? Thanks for the encouragement, bro!" Well, despite how it might look at first glance, David is not saying we are utterly incapable of decency and goodwill. As we learned in earlier devotions, the very first thing out of the Father's mouth after He created man was the prophetic declaration, "It is very good!" David isn't trying to contradict what God declared in Genesis 1. Instead the psalmist is referring to our righteousness (or lack thereof) apart from Christ.

So what is righteousness? Simply put, it's our right standing with God. When David says, "My goodness is nothing apart from you," he's saying there's no good behavior of his own that positions him rightly before the Father. Our righteousness is a gift that was purchased through the cross and given to us freely. Paul goes out of his way to drive this point home in Romans 1:17; 3:22, 26; 4:3, 5, 9, 13; 9:30; 10:4; Galatians 2:16; 3:6, 11; 5:5; and Philippians 3:9. And these are just a few of the many examples.

Our actions do not put us in good standing with God; our trust in Jesus imparts His righteousness to us. Righteousness isn't a fifty-fifty split between God's best effort and ours; it's an all-or-nothing deal. It's either all of Jesus' righteousness and none of our own, or no righteousness at all.

Why is all this theological talk of imputed righteousness so crucial to our everyday lives? Because many of us spend too much time and energy trying to open doors of favor on our own instead of resting in what God freely gives us.

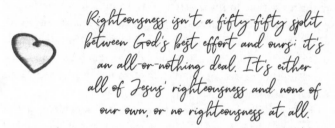

Righteousness isn't a fifty-fifty split between God's best effort and ours; it's an all-or-nothing deal. It's either all of Jesus' righteousness and none of our own, or no righteousness at all.

Job is an excellent example of this type of faulty religious thinking. Though Job's initial response to losing everything was rather impressive, the test of time revealed what was genuinely inside of him. When the days of suffering turned into weeks, he was forced to get honest with God. In Job 13:3 he cried out, "I would speak to the Almighty, and I desire to argue with God." Like a litigator arguing in a court of law, Job went on to present all of his good behavior and righteous actions as evidence that he did not deserve the suffering he was enduring. In his mind he was innocent, and bad things don't happen to good people.

I love the Father's response to Job's accusation. God doesn't answer him from a distance with an arm's-length air of aloofness; He draws near in a dramatic, seventy-plus-question, face-to-face encounter. And almost more intriguing than what God says to Job is what He leaves unsaid. The Father doesn't respond to a single one of Job's accusations. He doesn't take the stand and engage the argument of whether Job is righteous. The Father instead asks Job a series of questions that confront Job's transactional approach to Him.

Job was looking for self-vindication through an argument, but God was looking for a relationship through an encounter. Job was expecting God to explain His behavior, but God was longing to reveal His heart. God's questioning unearthed the realization that Job was attempting to uphold a standard of righteousness disconnected from a personal relationship with God, and that doesn't work. Job's biggest mental obstacle was that he couldn't understand how a righteous man could become the object of God's displeasure. But Job's faults weren't in his mind; they were in his heart.

Job's enlightenment after the encounter is evident in His response. "I have heard of You by the hearing of the ear; but now my eye sees You" (42:5). Before the trial Job had only heard of God; he hadn't seen Him face to face. God was just an impersonal force, a means to an end. In Job's limited understanding a blessed life was his for the taking as long as he fulfilled his end of the bargain by living righteously.

Job probably would have said that God's goodness opened the doors of favor over his life, but in reality Job believed his piety had gotten him where he was. God was like an ATM to Job. "If I insert my good behavior into the machine, God will pay up and bless me!" Job lived undisturbed in this narrow understanding for years while life was good, but when the "favor ATM" stopped spitting out dollar bills, it challenged everything he thought he knew. And thank God it did, because God's kindness shakes us from the stupor of self-righteousness.

Earlier in this book I shared how my immediate response to Lily's health crisis was to ask God what deep, dark sin I'd committed to stir His righteous anger against my family. The trauma and pain of the moment revealed that I held a viewpoint similar to Job's: surface level and transaction based. My response exposed a deeply held belief that my actions ultimately were the reason for blessings or trials in my life. In other words, if things are going great, it must be because of my behavior. But if my blessings go away, it must be because I failed.

This shallow approach to the Father's heart is exactly why He sent His Son, Jesus, to shift our paradigms concerning His nature. He wants to upend the tables in our minds. He wants to take this "religious detachment disorder" generation and flip it on its head. He came to free us from an unsympathetic system that, without revelation of His nearness, will eventually choke the life out of us.

So how do we walk through the door? Every good and perfect gift in our lives, from the salvation of our souls to the pack of Doublemint gum in our pockets, is all because of God's goodness. And the doorway to that goodness is Jesus. Jesus in Revelation 3:8 says, "I have put before you an open door which no one can shut," and in John 10:9 He says, "I am the door." Any door that we open through our own strength is not God's door. If we open the door ourselves, it can also be shut. But if God opens the door, no one can ever shut it.

But again, how do we walk through the door? Well, what do you do when someone holds a door open for you? You simply say, "Thank you," and walk on through! Psalm 100:4 tells us to "enter His gates with thanksgiving and His courts with praise." The courts in this verse represent the Father's nearness, and the gate is the way in. All you need is the password: "Thank You!"

There is something liberating about responding to every situation with thankfulness. It takes the onus off us. When we react with gratefulness to the gifts in our lives, we acknowledge that we are not the givers, just happy recipients. Thankfulness is so much more than a positive outlook on life. It is transformative and powerful in nature. It is effective in getting our stubborn egos out of the way, allowing us to walk into what Jesus has already offered: His righteousness.

Going Deeper

For it is You who blesses the righteous man, O Lord,
You surround him with favor as with a shield.
—Psalm 5:12

If you're like me at all, you may read a verse like this and wonder if it applies to you because you're not sure that you are righteous. Well, if you're worried about it, you probably have nothing to worry about! But seriously our righteousness comes from what Christ has done, not what we do. You are the righteousness of God in Christ (2 Cor. 5:21), and because of that you tend to act righteously. So receive the favor of God by thanking Him for it!

> Lord, You are truly gracious to me. I thank You that You surround me with favor, not because I deserve it but because Jesus purchased righteousness for me. I receive that, and I say, "Thank You." I receive favor surrounding me too. I live in Your favor as Your child. Thank You, Lord.

THE PERFORMANCE TRAP

Understanding the difference between healthy striving and perfectionism is critical to laying down the shield and picking up your life. Research shows that perfectionism hampers success. In fact, it's often the path to depression, anxiety, addiction, and life paralysis.
—BRENÈ BROWN

I AM A RECOVERING perfectionist. It's challenging for me not to think constantly about self-improvement, not to search incessantly for ways to be a better Christian, father, husband, friend—and the list goes on. But often the price of so-called perfection is everything. My joy and even my general contentment are often casualties in my pursuit of betterment. Some days it feels as if I've spent most of my life trying to impress God, as if all of my actions—from the moment I wake up until the moment I lay my head down—are just desperate attempts to get Him to notice how amazing I am.

Our value and purpose were never meant to derive from what we can accomplish, especially when our motivation is to be noticed by others.

This vicious cycle is what I've come to call "the performance trap," and it's the idea that we are defined only by what we can do. It keeps us running at breakneck speed, trying to make everyone happy—including God. The performance trap says that if we don't do everything for everyone all the time, there's a chance that they might not like us anymore; and if they don't like us anymore, we no longer have value or purpose.

Our value and purpose were never meant to derive from what we can accomplish, especially when our motivation is to be noticed by others. Congratulations from God and men are not commodities to be bought; they are received only by availing ourselves to one another in a loving relationship.

In my younger and more vulnerable days I even found myself trapped by my gifts. I tried to wield my natural talent as a singer and musician to impress God (and people). But with this mindset nothing is ever enough. It always keeps you wanting more. When you get the big stage you've always wanted, you long for a bigger one. When you write the hit song you've been plodding away at for years, you strive for another one that's bigger and better than before.

But the things of earth were never meant to satisfy the itch that eternity placed inside of us. As a young man I failed to realize that the gifts and talents God gave me were only ever meant to be vehicles into His presence—nothing more, nothing less. The beauty of being able to sing and lead worship was more about spending time with Him than impressing anyone with my skills. It was all leading to encounter, not to producing something that caused someone to marvel.

I want to pose a question that might ruffle some Western-minded, individualistic feathers: What if being OK with who we are is less about being concerned with what sets us apart (or what doesn't) and more about being conformed to the image of Christ? What if it's about losing ourselves in the reality of Christ in us, our hope of glory (Col. 1:27)? "I no longer live, but Christ lives in me" (Gal. 2:20, NIV). What if self-acceptance is about abandoning our personalities, preferences, and patterns of thought and fully taking on the mind of Christ? What if we could become windows into God's Father heart for others through our selfless actions? What if we could be living examples of reckless love to real people in our spheres of influence? I suggest that this is the only way to be truly content with ourselves in these seventy years on earth.

We must learn to see ourselves defined by what Jesus did on the cross instead of by what we can produce in our own strength. Grace requires nothing of us. God is all-powerful and already has everything; He owns the cattle on a thousand hills, as Psalm 50:10 says. But there's still one thing He desires—our surrendered hearts, given without pretense or façade.

When we realize He already accomplished everything at the cross, we no longer have to live by the requirements of the law. Law equals performance; grace equals rest. It's much easier to bring ourselves to the family table when we know we don't have to be perfect to have a seat in the first place. We can come as we are, trusting His promise that He won't let us stay that way because He's so fiercely devoted to our growth.

You see, sometimes I think we make the mistake of looking at ourselves through the lens of the performance trap. We see our shortcomings and scars and assume we're worthless because of them. But the truth is, He kisses our scars and reminds us that He makes all things new. He lifts our eyes to the cross, where His love takes our shortcomings and stretches them, just like His open arms, as far as the east is from west, making them forever enough. Are we willing to believe Him?

Going Deeper

Although "Reckless Love" appealed to a broad spectrum of people, it may have had special meaning to people like me who were stuck in the performance trap. God sang over me before I spoke a word, before I could earn it in any way. When I was His foe, He and His love fought for me. That's the furthest thing away from earning His love!

It's time to ponder the true motivations for your actions to see if you are trying to earn God's love. Be honest with yourself because that's the only way to get over performing for God.

+ **What are some things you do, consciously or subconsciously, to get in good with God?**

+ **What would it take for you to accept God's love for you and then do those same things *from* love instead of *for* love?**

So if the Son makes you free, you will be free indeed.

—John 8:36

THROUGH MY FATHER'S EYES

There is the person you think you are. There is the person
others think you are. And there is the person God knows
you are and what you can become through Christ.
—Billy Graham

Every Wednesday night is movie night at the Asbury
household, making it the kids' favorite evening of the
week by far (and a close second to steak night for me). There
is something special about our tradition of snuggling up in
the basement and enjoying a great story together—even if
that something special is just peace and quiet for two hours.
I'd like to personally thank Disney and Pixar for creating so
many classics that have become lasting memories in my family's heart. One of my favorites is the film *Inside Out*. I have
to admit, I'm an easy cry when it comes to movies. But I'm
pretty sure *Inside Out* set a record for most tears shed during
a two-hour period.

Since you've probably already seen it (and almost everyone
with kids has), I'll spare you a lengthy explanation of the
premise. Just know that the main characters aren't people, per
se. Instead they are personifications of five emotions belonging
to a young girl named Riley. Joy, Sadness, Fear, Anger, and
Disgust must all learn how to express themselves properly in
ways that are healthy for Riley's development into adolescence.

The entire movie subtly unpacks profoundly moving truths
that give insight into how God sees us, but the opening scene is
the one that got me. It begins from the perspective of newborn
Riley, opening her eyes for the first time, struggling to make out

the two blurry images in front of her. As her vision becomes clear, we see what becomes the first picture of her entire life— her father and mother beaming with delight, smiling from ear to ear. Riley's father lovingly declares, "Look at you. Aren't you a little bundle of joy?" As soon as Riley hears these words, her mind creates a memory like a snapshot. This memory serves as a deep anchor for the rest of her life.

Part of the reason I was "chopping onions" from the get-go was that it reinforced the significant impact my wife and I have on our kids when we express our love for them. But I knew there was something deeper to my tears.

Imagine, if you will for a moment, that you are Adam. (No, not your-next-door-neighbor Adam—the first-guy-ever-created Adam.) You don't enter the world as an infant; you appear out of nowhere as a full-grown man. (First of all, that's super weird and slightly disturbing, but it's God's design, so we can't argue with it, right?) The very first memory in your memory bank is when you were suddenly awakened by the breath of God (except you don't know He's God yet).

I don't know if you're anything like me, but I am incapable of thinking coherently when I first wake up in the morning, so I can't fathom how groggy and confused Adam must have been after waking up from *eternity* as a thought in the heart of God. While he's struggling to figure out what in the world is going on, Adam sees his Creator standing in front of him. Surely Adam was curious about what this unknown Being would say. It might have been natural for him to assume this all-powerful Creator would demand allegiance, saying something like, "I am your Master. Serve Me forever, or you will die!"

But this isn't at all how God starts the relationship. The first chapter of Genesis gives us the breakdown in verses

28–31. The Father blesses Adam by speaking purpose and calling over him. Then, to cap things off, God speaks to Adam's identity as a person: "It is very good," He says. Before God made Adam, God called the rest of creation "good." But after surveying the final brushstrokes of His masterpiece, He adds a "very" in front of that "good."

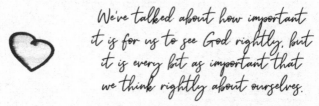

We've talked about how important it is for us to see God rightly, but it is every bit as important that we think rightly about ourselves.

From the moment the universe was fashioned, God made it clear who the crowning jewel of creation was. God went out of His way to make sure Adam saw himself the way God did. Like Riley opening her eyes for the first time and seeing her parents overwhelmed with delight for her, the Father wanted Adam to know that before he did a thing, he was unconditionally loved and accepted.

Just like God spoke blessing, calling, and identity over Adam, God wants to speak to the deepest places in you as well. We've talked about how important it is for us to see God rightly, but it is every bit as important that we think rightly about ourselves.

Psalm 139:17–18 says, "How precious also are Your thoughts to me, O God! How vast is the sum of them! If I should count them, they would outnumber the sand. When I awake, I am still with You."

I recently spent what felt like an entire afternoon vacuuming sand out of my truck after a day trip to Lake Michigan with my family. The amount of sand just from the bottom of my kids' feet was unimaginable. I couldn't help but call to mind Psalm 139. I decided to Google how many grains of sand were in a single seashore. Results varied, but one of them estimated that there are roughly ten thousand grains of sand in one cubic inch. When you multiply that by the millions of cubic inches that exist even in less than a mile of coastal beaches, you start to understand the staggering the truth of the psalmist's words. How vast is the sum of the Father's thoughts toward you! And Jeremiah takes things even a step further, letting us know that His thoughts toward us are not thoughts of harm, but of hope and a future (Jer. 29:11).

I have become obsessed with accessing the trillions of thoughts my Father is thinking about me at any given time. Knowing and believing what God thinks about me exposes the erroneous ideas manufactured in my mind for what they are: lies.

I take time in the middle of every day to ask my Father, "What do You think about me right now?" That's because if I do something I'm proud of, I think, "Man, I'm awesome." But when I fail, I think thoughts like, "I'm the worst. Why can't I ever get it right?" Without this daily exercise my thoughts would fluctuate with my circumstances. They would be tossed about dramatically like a ship lost at sea. But His thoughts toward me are like an anchor for my soul. In my success or failure they are the same.

Going Deeper

I encourage you to ask the Father what He thinks about you. Don't put words in His mouth. Just let Him speak to your heart. Start with what He already wrote to you in Scripture, and let those living and active words find you where you are.

Let Him declare blessing, calling, and identity over you. Here are a few thoughts God is thinking about you right now.

I have loved you with an everlasting love (Jer. 31:3).

I rejoice over you with singing (Zeph. 3:17, NKJV).

You're My treasured possession (Exod. 19:5, NIV).

All of My delight is in you (Ps. 16:3, HCSB).

+ **Take a quiet moment to sense what God is thinking or saying about you right now.**

+ **Imagine God leaning over and gazing at you when you were first born. What do you believe He would say as He looked at you?**

> For you created my inmost being; you knit me together in my mother's womb. I praise you because I am fearfully and wonderfully made; your works are wonderful, I know that full well.
>
> —PSALM 139:13–14, NIV

Keep this scripture with you today, and thank God today for the wonderful work that you are!

Day 19

YOU ARE "THE ONE"

God loves each of us as if there were only one of us.
—St. Augustine

*T*HE YEAR WAS 1995, and I was a dopey ten-year-old kid with an embarrassing bowl haircut waiting to check in for a local VBS (Vacation Bible School) program when I spotted a table full of stickers up ahead. The words "God Loves You" were proudly displayed on more than a hundred little labels. While it was a thoughtful gesture, the fact that every single camper in the school got the same "special" sticker left me feeling a little cheated.

"Well, great," I thought. "God loves me, but He loves everyone else just as much, so there's nothing special about me, and there's certainly nothing unique about the way He thinks about me compared to everyone else." Was it selfish of me to be hurt that God might love everyone equally? Probably. But I think something deeper was stirring in the heart of that out-of-place little kid. Something inside of me was yearning for a personal relationship with the Father that I didn't even know existed.

Years later, thankfully, I can laugh when I think of how shallow my childhood view of God's love was. I don't blame little miniature Cory for feeling what he felt. It's an endearing reminder of how far my relationship with God has come. Through joy and pain, laughter and tears, highs and lows, I've grown to understand that which no one can take from me: God's love for me isn't like His love for anyone else. While the Father's love for me might not be any more or less fervent compared to others, He does love me uniquely, and that's what matters. He set His sights on me when I was a lost sheep and chased me down until He found me. And the way He rejoices over me is like no one else.

Not only is the Father's love for each of us unique, but it's also immeasurable. To say that God loves everyone equally is, in my estimation, a gross misunderstanding of His unfathomable capacity for passion and adoration. Remember, God is love, and if God is love, there is no end to love because God has no end—He is infinite. And if love is infinite, it's impossible to place a metric on its reach or power. Being loved equally doesn't move my heart, but being loved infinitely—well, that's something altogether more mind blowing, especially when I consider the One doing the loving is the uncreated God of Genesis 1.

Over seven billion people currently live on earth. I don't know if you've ever stopped to think about it, but the fact that there are that many humans alive on the planet at one time blows my mind. That staggering number can cause us to feel small and insignificant. It's easy to think of ourselves as just a single square of toilet paper in a massive value-sized pack from Costco (bought at a discount, no less!) instead of the rare and beautiful work of God's hands that each of us is. The number of people alive today—plus the vast number of those who have gone before us—can cause us to feel as if we're just occupying a fraction of God's capacity for attention. But the Scriptures have a very different story to tell.

There is no part of His heart that He isn't longing to share with you.

In John 17:22–23 (NIV) Jesus prayed, "I have given them the glory that you gave me, that they may be one as we are one—I in them and you in me—so that they may be brought to complete unity. Then the world will know that you sent me and have loved them even as you have loved me." Take a second and let the weight of Jesus' words to the Father hit you. The boundless love that the Father had for Jesus from before time began He also has for you. God doesn't love in fragments or pieces. He only knows how to give all of Himself. He offers the fullness of His love.

That means there is no part of His heart that He isn't longing to share with you. The Father has no less delight in you during the mundane, day-to-day parts of life than He had for Jesus on the cross. We cannot grasp the magnitude and beauty of a love like that. God is the only Being in the universe who can love all of us fully without compromising His measure of passion for any of us. You don't have one seven-billionth of God's love; you have all of it. God doesn't think about you one in every seven billion seconds; you're always on His mind, both now and since the foundations of the world.

> When I look at your heavens, the work of your fingers,
> the moon and the stars, which you have set in place,
> what is man that you are mindful of him, and the son
> of man that you care for him?
>
> —PSALM 8:3–4, ESV

I love the wonder and praise that pours from David's lips in Psalm 8. He looks at the vastness of the universe, and instead of feeling unimportant and insignificant, he feels all the more valuable. Isn't it ironic how one person can think about the breadth of God's power displayed in the billions of planets in the galaxy and feel completely worthless, while another with the right perspective can ponder the same cosmos and feel fiercely loved? The two see the same things around them, but their views concerning the implications couldn't be more different. As incredible as nature is *around* you, it can't compare to the beauty of the love of God *in* you. The power displayed at creation when the Father spoke light into existence pales in comparison to the power of His love speaking illumination to your heart and mind. There isn't anything in the world more beautiful or awe-inspiring than His love poured out uniquely in each of us.

One of my heroes, the late Rich Mullins, spoke these words concerning the privilege of being loved by God: "I grew up hearing everyone tell me, 'God loves you.' I would say big deal, God loves everybody. That don't make me special! That just proves that God ain't got no taste. And I don't think He does. Thank God! Because He takes the junk of our lives and makes the most beautiful art."[1]

You are the one He loves. You are the one He adores. Your unique love was the joy set before Him at the cross. Your love was the dream of His heart in the garden, and it is the end goal in the new heavens and the new earth. God doesn't just tolerate you; He likes you. He appreciates your little quirks and idiosyncrasies—they set you apart from everyone else.

Going Deeper

If you've been on this planet for a few years, you've probably heard, "God loves you."

+ In the past what has been your emotional reaction to this statement? Did you receive it with joy, with a shrug of the shoulders, or with a touch of scorn?

+ While you were reading about how David saw the vastness of the sky and felt valuable to God, did you realize that there may be another way of thinking about how God loves you?

Yes, seven billion people live on this planet, and God loves each of us.

+ How does the infinite nature of God and His love help you understand that He can love each person uniquely without diminishing His love for anyone else?

The next time you look up at the night sky or press your toes in the sand on a beach, remember that you are unique to God and that He is able to love you both vastly and uniquely.

> Are not two sparrows sold for a penny? Yet not one of them will fall to the ground outside your Father's care. And even the very hairs of your head are all numbered. So don't be afraid; you are worth more than many sparrows.
>
> —Matthew 10:29–31, niv

STOP DOING AND START BEING

God is far more interested in what you are
becoming than what you accomplish.
—RICK WARREN

ARLIER THIS YEAR my family and I took a much-needed sabbatical to Dallas, Texas. For those of you unfamiliar with the concept of *sabbath*, we'll talk more about it in a minute. On a shockingly cold March Michigan morning Anna and I loaded the kids (and Sherlock, our new golden retriever pup) into our brand-new Chevy Tahoe. We'd bought this rig specifically for road trips, and boy, was it decked out with goodies. The DVD player, Bluetooth connectivity, and cruise control were only the tip of the iceberg. This upgraded vehicle was significant to me because I'd been driving a 1998 Toyota T100 pickup for twelve years or so prior to the new purchase. Needless to say, "The T" (as I affectionately referred to her) didn't exactly have state-of-the-art features like our new Tahoe. So we set out on the open road with bright eyes and bushy tails, believing that the time away would bring refreshment and restoration to our family.

There's something you don't know about me: I hate road trips. They are the bane of my existence. The tedium of sitting for hours and hours not doing anything drives me insane. I am an extremely driven person (no pun intended), so I'm always trying to speed things up in the name of efficiency. I've gotten many a speeding ticket in my day. I'm sure you're familiar with the navigation apps on your smartphone that give you an ETA for your destination. Well, I make it my mission in life to prove them wrong. If Google Maps tells me I'm supposed to get in at 9:30 p.m., I'll try my darnedest to get it down to 9:00 p.m. And when I get it down to 9:00 p.m., I'll start aiming for 8:30 p.m. It's a vicious cycle.

As is often the case with married couples, Anna is the exact opposite of me in this area—she loves road trips! She loves the slowness of the pace, the unhurried time for conversations, the countless hours staring out the window, pondering the meaning of life. But I think she loves the snacks and pit stops in all the different cities most of all. As hard as I try, I can't wrap my head around her love for exploration. We couldn't be more different from each other in this regard. My mantra is "Just get me there!" while hers is "As long as it takes."

Well, to be a good husband, I promised Anna I wouldn't complain about traffic, freak out about slow drivers in the left lane, whine about how many pee stops we were making, scream at people through the sunroof, or—I could go on, but I'll stop there. Suffice it to say, I promised her I'd try my best to slow down and enjoy the time together as a family, and that I'd consider the drive (all three days' worth, mind you) just as important as the destination.

You see, that's my problem. I get so focused on where I'm trying to go that I can't enjoy the process of actually getting there. My impatient nature wants to arrive as soon as possible, while God is mainly concerned about spending time together on the way there. It's the conversation, the life that happens on the road to Emmaus, that matters. That's what relationship is all about, but I'm quick to forget the essential things in my quest for greatness. I get so swept up trying to write a good story for myself that I neglect the real author of the story.

The reality is, if we each made a straight line to the end of our lives (whether we ever reached spiritual maturity or not), we wouldn't have anything to say about the journey: no bumps in the road, no highs, no lows, and nothing by which to remember His faithfulness. But God is found in the middle, in the bright darkness of faith. The middle is where Jesus reaches out His hand. It's in the dead of night when dawn's glow flickers unwavering in our minds. See, it's not about arriving at the finish line as quickly as possible; it's during the in-between moments of the race that the unseen shapes who we are.

After 2018 I was completely and utterly exhausted. The success of "Reckless Love" made it a massive year for my family and me. While I wouldn't change it for the world, it wasn't without its share of ups and downs. I'd done so many shows, concerts, award ceremonies, and radio events that about halfway through the year I realized something had to change. The Dallas sabbatical was a result of that desperation. Anna and I had been doing full-time ministry for twelve years straight with no breaks and very few vacations (because, as we discussed in an earlier devotion, it's tough to travel when you only make $1000 per month). Finally the sheer volume of God's roaring command to rest rose over the noise of our busyness, and for the first time in a long time we were all ears.

Sabbath comes from the biblical principle of *shmita*, which relates to agriculture and cultivation of land. According to Leviticus chapter 25, the Israelites were to take a yearlong break from working the land every seven years in order to preserve its fertility. When you study the implications of this principle, its depth of meaning is quite fascinating. God knew it was necessary for His people's sustainability. If the Israelites hadn't heeded God's command, their land would have dried up and ceased to produce fruit. Overworking would have zapped the life out of the soil. I think our lives are the same.

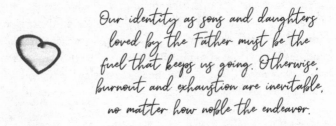

Our identity as sons and daughters loved by the Father must be the fuel that keeps us going. Otherwise, burnout and exhaustion are inevitable, no matter how noble the endeavor.

If all we do is work and work, eventually the soil of our lives gets depleted, and our ability to yield fruit shrivels. God knew what He was doing when He commanded the sabbatical year. He wants us fruitful for decades, not months. If our worth is based solely on what we can produce, then in our youthful zeal we will push ourselves too hard in too short a time, which causes burnout. We must stop doing and start being.

In Hebrew culture the Jewish day begins at nightfall. Therefore their days start with rest. They work from rest, not for it. Our Western culture is diametrically opposed to this concept. It tells us to grind hard and climb the corporate ladder in hopes of one day making enough money to retire for a few years before we die (bleak, I know, but pretty accurate). But that's not what God intended for us. He wants us to operate from a place of deep rest, fully alive in His love every day.

My friend Mike Bickle says, "A lover will always outwork a worker."[1] He means that a person motivated by love will end up doing far more for God than a person motivated by the principle of working hard. Our identity as sons and daughters loved by the Father must be the fuel that keeps us going. Otherwise, burnout and exhaustion are inevitable, no matter how noble the endeavor.

For me learning how to be instead of do means saying no to a lot of things, often really amazing things. The opportunities that have come my way since "Reckless Love" took off have been countless. However, with each one I hear the Father whisper, "Are you doing this to gain notoriety, or are you doing this from a place of rest?" My propensity to prove how cool and talented I am makes me want to jump at every invitation. But when I live from rest, knowing I'm already loved and accepted exactly as I am, I can weigh each opportunity with pure eyes and a pure heart. The power of my "no" is a force I am learning to wield with wisdom and in partnership with the Holy Spirit.

Going Deeper

Often, when we are feeling driven and out of control, we have moved out of God's rest into the place of making things happen on our own. Sometimes trusting God and resting in dependence on Him is the greatest fight of faith.

> Let us, therefore, make every effort to enter that rest.
> —Hebrews 4:11, niv

* Why do you believe we must "make every effort" to rest? Doesn't that sound like a contradiction?

* Why does resting in God go against our human (or sinful) nature?

* What one change can you make in your life today so you can do things from the place of rest?

> *Lord, it is easy for me to try to do things on my own, in my own strength and capability. Forgive me. I choose today to depend on You instead. I want to live in the*

rest You've provided out of Your great and perfect love for me. Remind me when I am making every effort except the effort to enter into Your rest. I trust Your love for me. Amen.

GETTING TO THE HEART OF THE MATTER

Day 21

AFTER GOD'S HEART

Whatever we behold or understand about God's heart toward us—that's what we become in our hearts toward God.
—MIKE BICKLE

A FEW WEEKS BACK some family friends graciously offered us their lake house for a few days. We had an amazing time together, swimming, fishing, and eating s'mores by the fire each night. As we were preparing to leave and doing a final cleanup, I noticed the vacuum I was using had tons of self-aggrandizing propaganda plastered all over it: "5-Star Rated!" "Never Loses Suction or Power!" "Lifetime Guarantee!" I laughed at the hilarity of the wildly over-the-top claims. However, they piqued my curiosity, so I decided to investigate further. I found that almost every product in the house was wrapped in similarly hyperbolic advertisements, as if the flattering words somehow added more intrinsic value to the product. In the end the main thing all these products had in common was that the big, bold proclamations emblazoned on them were invariably too good to be true.

What happens when the consumer sees through the hype of the labels? I certainly did. The vacuum I was using claimed it never lost suction, but I'll tell you, that thing couldn't pick up a finch feather covered in crazy glue. It was a joke. That's when I realized that we humans are often just like these products. We think we can fool everyone with our attractive labels and superficial displays of perfection. Our big, bold letters often read like, "Great human! Never messes up! Has a great, healthy family as seen on Instagram!" But the truth is, like the Rocket vacuum, we suck. The projections of greatness don't change who and what we are on the inside—broken and utterly incapable of fulfilling our purpose without God's help.

Jesus had a name for people who said one thing and did another: "whitewashed tombs...full of dead men's bones" (Matt. 23:27). He referred to this group of people as a "brood of vipers" (v. 33). Intense language for sure, but His thoughts toward the condition of their hearts were exactly that—intense.

In the letters to the seven churches in Revelation, Jesus indicted the church of Sardis for having a name or reputation for being alive but being dead on the inside (3:1). They were doing all the right things but had lost heart and passion somewhere along the way. How many of us say we are Christians but behave more like the world? How many of us put our best foot forward for the people who "matter," but live in the opposite manner when we think no one is watching? While this behavior borders on full-on hypocrisy, it's actually nothing more than a people-pleasing spirit birthed out of religious fear and striving. (Hint: Hypocrisy is saying you hold a particular set of beliefs while not even trying to live by their standards.)

Most of us would say we're followers of Christ who sometimes fail while reaching for His standard of holiness, not failures who sometimes succeed at loving God. Thankfully it's the intention and motive of the heart that count. And there's a big difference between hypocrisy and just plain weakness of the flesh. With God intention is everything when it comes to success or failure. Thank God, He doesn't see as man sees because usually, by the looks of things, I'm a mess.

The story of David's anointing as king of Israel in 1 Samuel 16 is a perfect example of the difference between God's perspective and man's perspective. Samuel arrived at Jesse's house under orders from the Lord to find and anoint the next king of Israel. In typical human fashion Jesse's sons were addressed from biggest to smallest, from most handsome to, well, least handsome. You see, they were operating by man's standard, according to the way things looked. But as Samuel started with the eldest son, God in His infinite wisdom disclosed His modus operandi: "Do not look at his appearance or at the height of his stature, because I have rejected him; for God sees not as man sees, for man looks at the outward appearance, but the LORD looks at the heart" (v. 7).

After Samuel had inspected all of Jesse's sons, he was sure the future king was not before him. Samuel asked if there was anyone else, almost insinuating that Jesse might have another son just lying around, someone so unimportant that he didn't even make the initial cut. Then, from the unseen, out-of-the-way recesses of the farm, David is called. When Samuel saw him, the Lord immediately told Samuel, "Rise and anoint him; this is the one" (v. 12, NIV). The most unlikely candidate from the most obscure place on his father's estate arose and stepped into his God-given calling as king of Israel that day.

But everything wasn't hunky-dory for David from then on. There were countless bruises and bumps along the way—some, no doubt, sustained to his physical frame from various battles, but infinitely more to his inner man from battles for his heart. See, God isn't out to hurt our pride; He's out to kill it. He uses even the most dismal of circumstances to cut to the heart of the matter. Among the more glaring of David's battles for the heart was his affair with Bathsheba and the subsequent murder of her husband. He did some other stupid things (like taking a census to prove his worth by numbering the people under his command as king), but the Bathsheba debacle takes the cake. I mean, to put it into perspective, imagine stealing your friend's wife and then sending him to die on the front lines of a war you should have been fighting. Not exactly a little white lie, huh?

God isn't out to hurt our pride; He's out to kill it.

To the naked eye (no pun intended), David was a murderous, adulterous, lying, stealing failure of a man, certainly not fit to be king and even more unfit to be called a man after God's own heart (Acts 13:22). However, God bestows the prestigious title upon him anyway. I believe the reason for this is simple: after all his blunders and transgressions, no matter how far from grace he fell, David maintained an unwavering devotion to God. Despite how deeply defeated he found himself, David never stayed there. He never wallowed in self-pity or camped out in regret and shame. He consistently ran back to the Father with reckless confidence, believing His kindness would always make a way for forgiveness and reconciliation. This is what made him a man after God's own heart.

Going Deeper

While most of us run away from God when we fall and attempt to hide our humiliation with religious fig leaves, David had the audacity to run to Him. Repentance was David's best friend. It was to him what the delete key on a keyboard is to us. With the simple press of a button, the mistakes go away; they disappear. That's the grace of God.

You don't have to hit any special key commands or type

any special access codes before pressing that delete key. Repentance that leads to forgiveness is always available to us. Seventy times seven, times seven, times seven, times a million, times infinity. That's the mercy of our God.

+ Describe a time when you experienced God's mercy.

+ Have you ever spent time seeking to know God's heart? How did it change your relationship with Him?

+ David wrote songs to express his feelings to God, and so do I. The Book of Psalms is a book of songs. Try writing a psalm describing what you've felt toward God.

WHAT HAS YOU STUCK?

What I hide, God cannot heal.
—STEVEN FURTICK

I was introduced to pornography at an early age, probably around twelve or so. That's a fun way to start today's devotional time, huh? I can picture many of you blushing in your armchairs right now.

As an eight on the Enneagram* I value truth, vulnerability, and straightforwardness above everything. For me there's no other way to go about this. I am vigilant to get stuff out in the open because I believe honesty before God and people is the first step toward true healing. Doing so gives me the strength to move forward in the affections of Christ.

Keeping things hidden in the dark is like leaving old milk in the fridge—it only gets fouler with time (which in turn exponentially increases our probability of neglecting it each day). We must confront our issues head-on, realizing that Jesus is not afraid of the ugly parts of our lives, the things we're too scared to let people see. He's already well acquainted with them, and He sees the end from the beginning and calls things that are not as though they were.

As I said, pornography was one of the ugly parts of my life for many years, even into my twenties after I had become a full-time worship leader. Because I couldn't bear the thought of anyone

---

* The Enneagram is an ancient system of nine personality types within the human psyche. You can find many online personality tests based on the Enneagram model. An eight is often characterized as a leader, challenger, and protector.

knowing that I, a minister of worship in the house of God, dealt with such a dark and evil thing, I couldn't confess it to anyone, which kept me in a perpetual cycle of guilt and shame. I was in a genuine Romans 7 quandary: the things I didn't want to do, I did; but the things I wanted to do, I couldn't do (vv. 14–20). I found myself completely and utterly stuck.

I got married when I was twenty-one years old. Anna and I were profoundly happy together, and I thought my happiness would cure my problem. Unfortunately I quickly found out that's not the way it works. Getting married doesn't magically fix all the problems in your life, especially the ones entrenched through years of habitual sin. The shame I felt from my struggle with pornography before marriage was nothing compared to what I experienced after. On top of hurting God's heart with my sin, I now mourned breaking my wife's heart as well—a double whammy of heartache. This burden was too much to bear.

To deal with the pain (and I do not recommend this), I put myself in what I now call "spiritual time-out." In this spiritual time-out I would, like the reverend in the *The Scarlet Letter*, flog myself continuously. However, my flogging wasn't with whips; it was with thoughts of self-hatred and condemnation. "How could you do this? Again?! You're the most repulsive human on the planet. God is disgusted with you." And the worst part was, the thoughts would intensify around the spheres of my calling and career. "You'll never write an anointed song. Your worship sets are going to suck because your life is full of hidden sin. You're nothing but a fake."

These time-outs would last days, sometimes weeks. In my mind, once I'd paid sufficient penance and abstained from sin for long enough, my anointing would return, and I'd feel good again. Even though I was always genuinely repentant, the cycle of hiding from God and punishing myself still ran like clockwork. In retrospect this belief system was not only ridiculous, but it was also unfounded biblically. Still, it ruled my life for years.

Then I got hold of the life of David. I resonated with his story big-time. I took solace in his public mess ups, thinking that if he could still be called a worshipper and a man after God's heart, surely I could as well. While pornography wasn't rampant in David's day the way it is in ours, the root problem, lust, still caused him to stumble into sexual sin a time or two—most notably with Bathsheba, as we talked about in yesterday's reading.

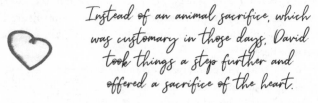

Instead of an animal sacrifice, which was customary in those days, David took things a step further and offered a sacrifice of the heart.

But I noticed something peculiar about David. After David became aware of his sin, he didn't force himself to endure months of self-flagellation. He didn't attempt to claw his way back into God's good graces through self-sacrifice and religious penitence. No, he threw himself wholly on the mercy of God, knowing that God wasn't after sacrifice and offering, but a broken and contrite heart. David knew that the inner world of the soul was paramount to God. After all David was the one passed over by his father because he didn't look the part but chosen by God because of his heart of gold.

At what should have been the lowest point of his life, David penned the words of Psalm 51.

> Have mercy on me, O God, according to Your
> unfailing love; according to your great compassion blot
> out my transgressions. Wash away all my iniquity and
> cleanse me from my sin....Cleanse me with hyssop,
> and I will be clean; wash me, and I will be whiter than
> snow. Let me hear joy and gladness; let the bones you
> have crushed rejoice....Create in me a pure heart, O
> God, and renew a steadfast spirit within me....Restore
> to me the joy of your salvation and grant me a willing
> spirit, to sustain me....You do not delight in sacrifice,
> or I would bring it; you do not take pleasure in burnt
> offerings. My sacrifice, O God, is a broken spirit; a
> broken and contrite heart you, God, will not despise.
> —Psalm 51:1–2, 7–8, 10, 12, 16–17, niv

Psalm 51 is one of the most famous psalms in scripture,
written after one of the most grievous transgressions. Notice
the boldness in David's words—almost commanding God
to heal him from his iniquity. Such was the confidence in
David's heart concerning the zeal of God to beautify His sons
and daughters, no matter how steeped in filth they might be.
Instead of an animal sacrifice, which was customary in those
days, David took things a step further and offered a sacrifice
of the heart. His sacrifice of praise was precious in the eyes of
the Father, and far more meaningful than the blood of bulls
and goats.

David didn't let his failure define him; he allowed his
Father to do that. And as we know, the words bestowed upon
David were enviable: a man with a heart like God's. David
severed the head of the giant of shame in one decisive blow by
boldly running to the throne of grace, even though he knew
he deserved the gallows of death. He defied religious logic to

create a new and better way, moving from a sacrifice wrought with mess and blood to a sacrifice of the heart offered in purity.

Going Deeper

I know it's counterintuitive. It makes no sense that the way to get rid of guilt and shame and sin is to run to the very One you offended—God. The natural human response is to hide like Adam and Eve did. But freedom comes from running to God instead.

- ✦ As I was talking about my issue with pornography, did something come to your mind that you beat yourself up over?
- ✦ I know that I have a straightforward personality, and not everyone is like me. But what would it take for you to run to God just as you are and confess everything to Him? How desperate would you have to become? What would lead to that kind of desperation?

My best suggestion to you is, don't wait until you're that desperate, because it probably means that something tough has happened to get you there. Right now, right where you are, start talking to God about this.

Open your Bible and pray Psalm 51 to God as if you wrote it. Pray from your heart and watch to see how God meets you right where you are.

FACE YOUR FEARS

Embrace uncertainty. Some of the most beautiful chapters in our lives won't have a title until much later.
—Bob Goff

*D*o you remember what life was like when you were young and everything was easy? That was before the stress and anxiety of adulting came on like a flood. I can recall carefree days spent playing games in elementary school with my friends. The classics of my childhood were Heads Up Seven Up, the Telephone Game, and Duck, Duck, Goose. It sure was nice when the hardest part of my day was finding an open seat when my classmates yelled, "Goose!"

But the one game I found difficult to endure was the Opposite Game. In that game, when someone shouted a word, you had to shout the opposite. "Awake"…"Asleep!" "Laughing"…"Crying!" "Hot"…"Cold!" This little educational game was supposed to help kids expand their vocabularies. But for me the subjective nature of the game always rubbed me the wrong way. See, I was both precocious and emotional at that age. Since I had a great love for words, I made it a point never to settle for the status quo reply. If someone said, "Hot," I said, "Lukewarm" or "Tepid." When it was my turn to suggest a word, I always chose one that didn't have an exact opposite to throw people off—something like *cacophony* or *antidisestablishmentarianism.*

Love isn't love unless it is expressed. Fear isn't fear unless it suppresses.

If you shouted out, "Love," in most settings kids would reply with "Hate." But the Bible proves that I wasn't that weird of a kid after all, because the opposite of love, according to 1 John 4, isn't what most people would think. Love's greatest enemy is not hatred; it's fear (v. 18). Does love cast out hate? Absolutely. But hatred isn't the root of what stifles love; fear is. While hatred can certainly germinate in a void of lovelessness, the only reason for the emptiness in the first place is that fear silenced love.

It's important to remember what we talked about before: love requires action. Love isn't love unless it is expressed. Fear is the exact opposite. Fear isn't fear unless it suppresses. Love moves forward; fear stays back. Love gives away; fear holds on. Love offers its heart; fear closes it off. Love accepts; fear rejects. In every moment, in every circumstance, both large and small, we have the choice to act in love or fear. If we want to be free from the prison of fear, love is the key. Perfect love is the only thing that can drive it out.

> There is no fear in love; but perfect love casts out fear, because fear involves punishment, and the one who fears is not perfected in love.
>
> —1 John 4:18

I can't tell you how many times I've attempted to overcome fear by gritting my teeth and doing my best to rise above it. But that never works because all actions devoid of love are powerless to free us from the paralyzing prison of fear. Whether we operate from fear or love, it reveals whom we trust.

So how do we face our fears? We face them not by ignoring them but by fixing our eyes on a higher power, the power of love.

> In the year that King Uzziah died, I saw the Lord sitting on a throne, high and lifted up, and the train of His robe filled the temple.
>
> —ISAIAH 6:1, NKJV

Allow me to give you some context for this passage. King Uzziah's death would have been terrifying for Isaiah. Have you ever noticed what happens to a nation when it enters an election season? Fear dominates the news cycles almost as thoroughly as it dominates the hearts of the people in the land. Change is difficult for people, no matter the time period in which they live.

Now imagine that your nation isn't transitioning to a new person who will lead for the next four to eight years; it's shifting power to the man or woman who's going to run the country for possibly the next seventy! To up the stakes, Isaiah the prophet will speak directly with the king on a regular basis. If the next king of Israel is good, Isaiah is A-OK. But if the next king is evil, not only is Israel's future at stake but so is Isaiah's life!

This realization would have undoubtedly filled Isaiah with great fear. So what was God's answer? He took the prophet's eyes off his circumstances and showed him who was really in control by allowing him to see the Lord on His throne. What had seemed insurmountable just moments before suddenly looked weak and powerless compared to the majesty, love, and power of the Almighty. A little perspective can change everything.

What do you do when you feel afraid? Here are three steps I recommend.

1. Acknowledge it. Feeling scared isn't wrong. It is an emotion we all experience. Fear only becomes harmful when you let it take residence in your heart and mind. It doesn't do any good to pretend nothing is happening. Recognizing the fear is half the battle.

2. Identify it. If fear is in you, some lie probably held the door open for it to enter. If you're courageous enough to face your fear, with the Father's help you will also see the lie the enemy planted to gain access.

   When I feel fear creeping in, I ask the Father, "Why am I feeling this right now?" Time and time again He has been faithful to help me identify the lie I'm believing. For example, if I'm experiencing fear of the future, the Father might whisper something like, "You are fearful because you don't trust Me as your provider."

3. Replace it. Now that you've recognized your fear and identified the lie that's driving it, you must replace that lie with the truth. You can't simply manage fear—you have to replace it with love. Before Isaiah could fix the issue, he had to replace the lie behind his fear with the truth of God's sovereignty.

Paul wrote to Timothy that "God has not given us a spirit of fear, but of power and of love and of a sound mind" (2 Tim. 1:7, NKJV). Why did the apostle single out these three gifts of God as the antidote for fear? I believe it was for the following reasons:

Power = God is stronger than fear.

Love = God's love takes the place of fear.

Sound mind = This is the result of choosing God's love.

As a final note I give you permission to stop being so hard on yourself. If you consistently deal with fear, it's not because you aren't saved or submitted to the love of God. Give yourself grace. It's a process.

Sometimes "perfect love" doesn't look or act the way we think it should. Sometimes it feels as if its effects aren't swift or decisive enough. I used to condemn myself with thoughts like, "If perfect love casts out fear, why do I still have pockets of fear in my life? Why hasn't fear gotten the eviction notice yet?" I'm learning that as love takes hold of the human heart, sometimes it's more like a slow crowding out of the old fearful way of thinking rather than a quick, clean sweep—more like a changing of the guard.

I think of it this way: when Steve Jobs created the iPhone, he didn't force people to buy it. He didn't buy up every other cell phone company or try to bankrupt them. He just sat back and allowed a "better way" to take hold. If love came in and made us perfect in one day, we'd wind up arrogant, forgetting our need for God. He's not so focused on our arrival that He ignores the in-between times—the unhurried meanderings, the rabbit trails of divine discovery, the occasional wrong turn—on the path to our final destination: home.

Going Deeper

If fear weren't a part of the human experience, God would not have told us so many times in the Bible to "fear not." He understands the precarious nature of our lives on earth because Jesus lived among us and felt what we feel.

• **Think about a fear you regularly face. Have you ever acknowledged it? Why or why not? Is that something you could do today?**

Now identify that fear and ask God why you run into it often. See if God shows you a door that allowed it in, perhaps a past experience or a past wound.

Now is the time to be brave and replace that fear with the truth from God's Word. What does the Bible say about the situation in which you usually feel fear? Declare that over your mind and feelings and life.

Remember that God's perfect love casts out fear. Lean into His love for you as you face your fears.

> *Father, thank You that Your perfect love casts out fear. I choose to fear not today, because You are with me. I lean on You. Thank You, Lord.*

FAILURE, THE BIGGEST FEAR OF ALL

Stop allowing your fear of getting it wrong to color
every beautiful thing you're doing right.
—RACHEL HOLLIS

Like the other seven billion people on the planet, I deal with fear—the fear of failure, to be more exact. I constantly worry about failing others, failing myself, and most of all, failing God. I know it doesn't matter in the broad scope of things, but for some reason the thought of coming up short in any area of my life makes me feel like less of a person.

A key passage of Scripture that has helped me in the battle against fear is 2 Corinthians 12. The author, Paul, was an impressive man by any standard. He hailed from a distinguished family and came up under the most prestigious education. He was a brilliant thinker and an even better leader. Paul was the type of guy who had it all. Still, underneath the brilliant thoughts and eloquent words, Paul struggled like the rest of us. He opened up about his wrestling in verses 7–10 (ESV):

> So to keep me from becoming conceited because of the surpassing greatness of the revelations, a thorn was given me in the flesh, a messenger of Satan to harass me, to keep me from becoming conceited. Three times I pleaded with the Lord about this, that it should leave me. But he said to me, "My grace is sufficient for you, for my power is made perfect in weakness." Therefore I will boast all the more gladly of my weaknesses, so that the power of Christ may rest upon me. For the sake of Christ, then, I am

content with weaknesses, insults, hardships, persecutions, and calamities. For when I am weak, then I am strong.

The most interesting thing to me about this passage is that Paul doesn't provide any clarity concerning the nature of the thorn. We only know that it weakened him significantly, most likely making him more susceptible to failure. Scholars have debated over the years whether his thorn was a speech impediment, a physical ailment, a temptation, persecution, or something altogether more bizarre. Yet Paul doesn't even consider the details of his weakness significant enough to delineate. He does, however, give us a pivotal revelation for overcoming fear of failure: not only is God undeterred by weaknesses and failures, but in accordance with who He is as eternal Redeemer, He uses them as opportunities to perfect His strength. He's not afraid of our failure. It might be more accurate to say He's drawn to it.

A few years ago I found myself feeling nervous about leading worship at a big conference. This was unusual for me because I hadn't gotten butterflies before an event in a long time, regardless of how big or important it was. I'm not sure whether it was the anxiety of other circumstances surrounding my life or the blazing hot wings I had eaten right before bed, but that night I couldn't sleep a wink.

Not only is God undeterred by weaknesses and failures, but in accordance with who He is as eternal Redeemer, He uses them as opportunities to perfect His strength.

My stress level seemed to rise with every passing second as I tossed and turned restlessly in bed. I felt fear start to creep in, whispering that I wouldn't be at my best the next day and everyone would know it. Visions of disaster played out in my mind like horror movies and crowded out my usual air of peace. I imagined my voice cracking at the climax of the big song, forgetting the crucial lyric when it mattered most, or just passing out mid-set from sheer exhaustion.

At 4:00 a.m., only three hours before I had to leave for the venue, I crawled out of bed and decided to lay on the couch in an attempt to trick my body back to sleep. I put on a familiar worship album in hopes that the soothing sounds would help me wind down. A couple of bars into the first song, I felt the Father invite me to engage in worship at that very moment. I raised my hands and started singing along, tears rolling down my face as I lay flat on my back on that grey faux-leather hotel sofa.

After a few songs the anxiety began to creep back in, and I shifted from restful worship to frenzied supplication, begging God to let me fall asleep so the event would still be a success the next day. My prayers quickly turned plaintiff. "Why can't I sleep? Will I ever sleep again?" I pleaded as the tears poured. (Hey, I was tired. Give me a break, OK?) "Why would You do this to me? Don't You know I won't be able to be at my best tomorrow?" I didn't hear a direct answer to my questions, but God did speak something to my heart at that moment. "Cory, I love how leaned into Me you are. I love how dependent you are on Me right now."

I felt fear retreat as the love of the Father held me. Just moments before He spoke, my anxiety was so intense it felt as if I were drowning. But when He whispered that simple phrase, it was like the glass enclosure around me shattered, the water gushed out, and I could breathe again.

I was only anxious in the first place because I was afraid of being seen as weak. I was fearful the crowd would see right through me and think less of me because of my poor performance. Instead of seeing my weakness as an opportunity for Him to reveal His strength, I wanted my own strength to be on display. I had lost sight of why I was leading worship in the first place—to bring glory to God. It's not that I intentionally wanted to steal His glory, but I wanted to do well so the Father would be proud of me and so people's lives would change for the better.

But in that moment on the hotel couch, suffocating in fear's death grip, His love changed everything. He didn't wait to reveal His love until I was at full strength. He wanted me to experience it right there amid my failure so I would remember how to be leaned into His love.

The worship service wasn't noticeably or outwardly different the next morning, but there was a distinct difference in me. This time I remained reliant on God's grace from start to finish—not just when I felt weak, but when I felt strong as well. While I don't believe God inflicts sleeplessness on His people, I do believe He used it that night to remind me that He doesn't just love me when I get it right. He loves me when I mess up, when I'm frail, and when I'm needy. God prefers that I lead in physical weakness while depending on His love rather than operate at the height of my talent and gifting without relying on Him.

To overcome the fear of failure, you must recognize that when you are weak, He is strong. Your weakness is not repulsive to Him; He's drawn to it like a magnet. He can't help but come running when His kids cry out! If we never failed, we would never need God. Failure isn't just a fear to overcome; it's a beautiful reminder of our need for God, a God who doesn't require perfection for love.

Your imperfections allow His love to shine through you; they're like the cracks through which His light pours out to a dark and destitute world. Next time you're feeling bummed about yourself, remember these words: God's got a soft spot for weakness, and I'm the weakest of them all!

Going Deeper

The fear of man has paralyzed many of us at different times. The moment we feel that we may lose face or have a failure exposed, we can easily succumb to fear. Yet I am saying that living with God in that weakness is more valuable that succeeding all day long because it causes us to lean on God and be made strong with His strength.

- Have you ever felt the strength of God during a very weak time? What was it like? How did God show up?

- Which part of my story did you relate with the most? How do you have a new view of failure now?

- What will you do next time you face failure?

Pray this scripture as you give your failures to God.

> Whom have I in heaven but You? And besides You, I desire nothing on earth. My flesh and my heart may fail, but God is the strength of my heart and my portion forever.
>
> —PSALM 73:25–26

Day 25

WHEN YOU'RE DEALING
WITH DEPRESSION*

I find myself frequently depressed...and I find no better cure for
that depression than to trust in the Lord with all my heart.
—CHARLES SPURGEON

O F ALL THE fictional figures, icons, and heroes to choose
from, Sherlock Holmes is my favorite character by
far. I know you will probably think I'm lame because of my
choice, but something about the way the Baker Street detective sees things no one else can resonates with me. I love the
thrill of piecing together the clues to crack the case. I love it
so much that, much to the chagrin of my wife, when we watch
the BBC series, *Sherlock*, I always solve the mystery before the
show reveals "whodunit" (followed by my extensive and bois-
terous bragging).

My favorite quote from Sherlock Holmes—and one that
he frequently employs in biting, British fashion, no less—is,
"You see, but you do not observe." The point that Holmes is
trying to make is that in all of life's circumstances, it is necessary to look not only at the obvious but also deeper into
the hidden elements that lie just beyond the surface. In most

---

* Today's devotional discusses what to do in moments of depression
or anxiety. It is crucial to understand the difference between a season
of grief, sorrow, or sadness and clinical depression. If you suspect that
you struggle with depression or anxiety, especially if you have thoughts
of harming yourself or someone else, seek professional help. There are
many reasons for depressive disorders, but there is no reason to feel
shame or guilt about getting the help you need.

situations the evidence seen by all isn't what breaks the case; it's the clues most people miss that change everything.

Now, when we're dealing with moments of depression or anxiety, I don't believe the Father takes an arrogant, know-it-all kind of posture like Detective Holmes. He's not impatiently waiting for us to crack the case so He can shame us with a cold phrase like, "You saw, but you did not observe." But, like Sherlock's bread and butter, I believe the Father opens our eyes to things that would have otherwise gone unnoticed. This is the method by which He delivers us from our personal valleys of depression and anxiety. He is gracious and compassionate; He sits and weeps with us when we're hurting. God draws near to the broken but doesn't leave them there. He always provides a way out, a path forward.

Hebrews 11:1 (NKJV) says, "Now faith is the substance of things hoped for, the evidence of things not seen." To me "evidence of things not seen" sounds like a self-contradicting statement, an impossible paradox of sorts. But many biblical accounts make spiritual sense of what looks like a natural discrepancy.

One example is Elisha's being surrounded by the Syrian armies in 2 Kings 6:14–17 (NKJV).

> Therefore [the King of Syria] sent horses and chariots and a great army there, and they came by night and surrounded the city. And when the servant of the man of God arose early and went out, there was an army, surrounding the city with horses and chariots. And his servant said to him, "Alas, my master! What shall we do?"
>
> So he answered, "Do not fear, for those who are with us are more than those who are with them." And

Elisha prayed, and said, "Lord, I pray, open his eyes that he may see." Then the Lord opened the eyes of the young man, and he saw. And behold, the mountain was full of horses and chariots of fire all around Elisha.

In this passage Elisha's servant tried to use his natural eyes to find spiritual evidence. Because he fixated on the problem instead of the solution, fear and heaviness incapacitated his heart. Elisha, on the other hand, chose a different method: faith. Like a good detective searching for the best evidence available, Elisha found substance in hope. The prophet didn't deny that a problem existed. Instead he denied the problem a place of authority in his mind. The visible reality of the situation was that Elisha and his servant found themselves surrounded by an army eager to make them into human pin cushions. But the greater reality, though invisible, was the presence of a mighty angel army surrounding the Syrians. Through faith Elisha found evidence of things not seen and chose to align his inner world with that faith.

This story might not connect immediately as a remedy for depression, but it has served as my life raft in storms of sadness. I see myself in both characters. Like the servant I usually feel overwhelmed and hopeless, staring solely at the armies of circumstance surrounding me. I fixate on the bleakness of the evidence all around instead of the solution. But I'm also like Elisha. Even when I lose sight of hope, I know God hasn't. His eyes see a favorable outcome to each story even when my eyes are blind.

Faith is the platform upon which we can become more than who we are (like Sherlock Holmes, Wonder Woman, Atticus Finch, or Princess Leia—whoever floats your boat).

It's the evidence all around us of things unseen—the proof of the Father's tender reach into our everyday lives. When we have eyes to see as the Father sees, we can envision ourselves lifted from the miry clay of anxiety and depression. Faith isn't phony or inauthentic; it's not something you conjure up on your best day. No, faith is merely surrendering to a higher power, the power of God's staggering love for us, and choosing to live accordingly.

David, despite his astonishingly well-chronicled past of depression, gives us a key to stepping into preposterous faith in Psalm 100:4 (NKJV): "Enter into His gates with thanksgiving, and into His courts with praise." Thankfulness is the blueprint. It isn't just a passive posture that we try our best to maintain in spite of our horrible lives. It is profound and powerful.

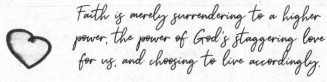

Faith is merely surrendering to a higher power, the power of God's staggering love for us, and choosing to live accordingly.

Allow me to demonstrate the power of thankfulness through a car analogy. (I apologize in advance to the mechanically impaired.) A car has two energy sources: the battery and the gasoline. The more powerful of the two, gasoline, creates an explosion inside your engine that generates such a significant amount of energy, it can propel a two-ton hunk of metal at speeds exceeding one hundred miles per hour. But gasoline's energy can't be accessed instantly; it needs another source to catalyze the combustion process. This is where the battery comes in. The battery doesn't have enough power to get your car to high speeds, but it does have something gasoline requires—instant energy. Thanks to the battery, whenever you turn the key, you have immediate energy that kick-starts the powerful combustion process of the gasoline, which gets you to where you need to go.

In this analogy thankfulness is the car battery, and faith is the fuel. Faith is powerful, yes, but because of the nature of the human spirit, it's often difficult to skip ahead in the process to the place of great faith without a few other steps. Thankfulness is like turning the key in the ignition; it kick-starts us to the place where faith can take over and do the rest.

When the armies of depression and anxiety surround me, it's nearly impossible for me to see the courts of praise, but I always have instant access to thanksgiving. No matter how confused or heavy I may feel, I must remember all the things for which I'm thankful. As I speak out in a spirit of gratefulness, like Elisha and his servant my eyes are opened to see that God hasn't left me. When I magnify the Lord through thankfulness, things suddenly come into proper perspective. Big things start to look big, and little things look little.

Going Deeper

We have all had times—especially nights—when situations loomed larger and more foreboding in our minds than they really were. Then we are tempted to imagine the worst possible outcome. In our minds we are showing up at the ER or planning a funeral. Yet those outcomes rarely happen.

Thankfulness is an antidote to falling into anxiety and depressing thoughts. It takes courage, though, to speak words of gratefulness when your mind is full of anxious thoughts.

+   Have you ever successfully outmaneuvered anxiety or depression by practicing thankfulness? What happened?

+   How can you remember to kick-start yourself to the place of faith in God through being (loudly) thankful the next time you face depressing thoughts?

> If the LORD had not been my help, my soul would soon have dwelt in the abode of silence. If I should say, "My foot has slipped," Your lovingkindness, O LORD, will hold me up. When my anxious thoughts multiply within me, Your consolations delight my soul.
>
> —PSALM 94:17–19

WHEN YOU FEEL REJECTED BY GOD OR OTHERS

Every time you think you're being rejected, God's actually redirecting you to something better. Ask Him to give you the strength to press forward.
—NICK VUJICIC

SOMETIMES I THINK this generation is too dramatic (myself included). For example, the other day I overheard a young man at a coffee shop emoting to his friend about how he's dealing with "intense rejection." I expected what followed to be something like his parents kicked him out of the house and disowned him because he forgot to take out the trash or he lost his high-paying job because of his hair color or something equally absurd. But no, his reason for "intense rejection" was that a friend of his hadn't responded to his text message from the day before. I wanted to throw my head back and laugh hysterically at him, but I didn't...because I'm a good Christian. Instead I just chuckled to myself and pondered all the times I'd overreacted to insignificant things in my own life.

See, I'm the type of guy who feels as if God has abandoned me when my fantasy football team isn't performing well or when I grab a pack of gum and there are only empty wrappers left. I bemoan the day I was born over trivial things like that. As I said, I lump myself in with this overdramatic generation. But what happens when real life strikes and we face situations that cause us to question where God is in all of it?

I imagine Joseph, the son of Jacob, had as many of those moments as any human ever has. If you're familiar with his story, you know it's the stuff that movies are made of nowadays. It's got more ups, downs, twists, and turns than all the roller coasters in North America combined.

Joseph was "called" at a young age (or at least he thought he was). God gave him multiple dreams concerning the brilliance of his future, and I imagine he was pretty high on life. I mean, dreaming that your brothers (all older, mind you) bow down before you must be a pretty good feeling, especially when you've been their punching bag for years. Joseph's life was on an upward trajectory. All he had to do was follow the neon signs the Father was giving, and great things were right around the corner.

It turns out, the only thing around the corner was betrayal. In an act fueled by carnal jealousy, Joseph's brothers left him in a pit to die. Honestly, while they took things too far, I can understand where they were coming from. Joseph, in his immaturity and arrogance, had a habit of flaunting his calling and his belovedness in front of his brothers. So, in a way, Joseph was partly responsible for his premature demise (he was also responsible for some of the first haters in biblical history). In Genesis 37:19 (NIV) they deride, "Here comes that dreamer!" Shortly after, his brothers hatch a plan to get rid of him forever. You see, haters always conspire to kill dreamers, but dreams from God never die.

Stranded and alone in a pit in the middle of the wilderness, I'm sure Joseph felt as if his dreams got flushed down the toilet. I can hear him pleading with God, "But You gave me these dreams! Why would You take them away?!" All the promises, but none of the follow-through. He must have felt staggering rejection. But as Joseph later learns, our God-given dreams are not meant to serve merely as badges of God's favor on our lives; they are intended to prepare us to serve in His kingdom humbly and without entitlement.

Joseph's redemption story is as meandering as it is hard to fathom. He is sold into slavery and winds up in Egypt in the house of a man named Potiphar. Even in a foreign land God's hand of favor is still on him, and that favor combined with his integrity promotes him to a place of leadership in Potiphar's household.

Potiphar's wife takes an interest in Joseph and tries to coerce him to sleep with her. He refuses, and she falsely accuses him of attempted rape, for which he spends many years in prison. Being falsely accused and punished for something as heinous as rape is an injustice I can hardly begin to grasp, yet Joseph's faith remains unwavering.

Eventually Pharaoh's cupbearer and baker end up in the same prison as Joseph. By interpreting their dreams, Joseph tells each one his future: one will live and one will die. Joseph begs the cupbearer (the one who lives) to remember him and mention him to Pharaoh so he can be exonerated, but the cupbearer forgets. Can you believe it? The cupbearer forgets. Genesis 41 tells us it's two long years before the cupbearer finally remembers Joseph's request. I don't know about you, but I wouldn't have lasted two days in an Egyptian prison, much less two years.

But somehow Joseph holds on to God's promises over his life. In a miraculous turn of events Joseph is released from prison to interpret Pharaoh's troubling dreams, which he does with pinpoint accuracy—something no one else in all the land could do. He is subsequently placed as second in command over all of Egypt.

God's promise to us isn't that everything will be easy but that He'll be with us even when it's not.

In a redemption story second to none God uses the sum of Joseph's trials and misfortunes to save his entire family from famine just a few years later. You can't make this stuff up—it's like something straight out of *The Count of Monte Cristo*. God truly takes what the enemy meant for evil and turns it for good, as Genesis 50:20 says.

God's promise to us isn't that everything will be easy but that He'll be with us even when it's not. Through the fires of rejection and mistreatment, Joseph remained unoffended. We can too. The weight of gold forged in Joseph's heart through the testing was more than all the multiplied wealth of the world. Joseph's life is a lesson to us that even when it feels as if the world is against us, even when God seems light years away, even when our cry of anguish is all we can hear, God's hand of favor is still upon us. Like the tides that etch themselves into the beautiful Cliffs of Moher in Ireland, we must learn to embrace even the waves that dash us against the rocks. In the dashing, His faithfulness is written on the tablets of our heart.

Going Deeper

Rejection is powerful because it cuts to your very identity, to the core of who you are. That's why it feels so deadly. But when your identity is rooted deeply in Christ, no one and no circumstance can shake you from the foundation of who you are in God.

♦ Joseph maintained an excellent spirit in the midst of all the unfair treatment he endured. How did you react the last time you felt rejection or were treated unfairly?

♦ God uses the waves that dash us against the rocks to make us ready for the dreams He has for us. How can believing that help you get through the next round of rejection you might face? What will you actively do to remind yourself you are still in God's favor when rejection comes?

You are God's, and His hand is on you through everything.

> Then Joseph said to his brothers, "Come close to me." When they had done so, he said, "I am your brother Joseph, the one you sold into Egypt! And now, do not be distressed and do not be angry with yourselves for selling me here, because it was to save lives that God sent me ahead of you.
>
> —Genesis 45:4–5, niv

WHEN YOU FEEL GOD HAS ABANDONED YOU

It's not too late. We're never too far....God is
always good, and he always remembers us.
—LOUIE GIGLIO

AFTER BOTH PREGNANCIES with our first two children, my wife dealt with severe postpartum depression. With Gabriel, our firstborn, it lasted about nine months. With Lily, our second, it was more severe, and almost a year passed before she started to feel like herself again. There were many dark, hopeless mornings when it felt as if we'd never find our way to the other side. Anna often woke up with what I can only describe as a cloud of blackness over her mind and emotions.

Usually, instead of settling into the hopelessness, she chose to sing, pray, or call a friend. I always knew my wife was a fighter, but these moments of unwavering devotion to God and her family convinced me I'd married a warrior. She would often ask me to tell her things (that didn't make sense to me at the moment) like, "You're not alone" and "You won't always feel like this." While I always thought it was silly that she wanted to hear things she already knew, I told her anyway. Any glimmer of hope in the dark hole she felt lost in was welcome, no matter how it came. If there was ever a time in our lives we dealt with the lie of abandonment, it was then.

As I've mentioned in other portions of this book, our daughter Lily went through some major life-threatening health issues. Unfortunately these two circumstances coincided. We were in what felt like the perfect storm (from hell), with Anna battling debilitating postpartum depression and our daughter fighting for her life.

Right around this time Sarah and John Mark McMillan released their song, "King of My Heart." The truths in the lyrics were anchors for our hearts. The resounding declarations, "You are good!" and "You're never going to let me down!" gave us the language of faith we needed to declare a greater reality than the one we were living. We had almost lost sight of those truths in our weariness. We latched onto the song as if our lives depended on it and began singing and leading it with a renewed fight in our souls. Anna faced head-on the lie that the Father had forsaken her. This song became her shield and buckler. She sang it and prophesied it until she believed with resilient conviction that God had not left her on her own.

At first the words seemed too good to be true. Our situation felt so dark and difficult; how could we possibly believe that God was good? Still, we chose to sing despite our circumstances. Even when we weren't entirely convinced that the words were true, we sang, and the more we sang, the louder we heard His love roaring above the lies. Even in the midst of great trials, when we felt as if God were a million miles away, He was still good, and His plans for us were full of hope, life, and deep joy.

In Deuteronomy 31:6 the Father made the everlasting promise that He will never leave us or forsake us. In this text the word *leave* refers to His presence, and the word *forsake* refers to His heart posture toward us. We all know you can be physically present with others in a room but have your heart closed off to them. For example, though Judas was with Jesus as one of the twelve disciples, his heart had already turned away from Jesus in betrayal. What the Father promises in this scripture is His undivided, uncompromising devotion to us. His heart will ever be leaning in toward us. He will never give up on us, never turn His back on us, and never leave us. He will always lay His heart out on the line for us.

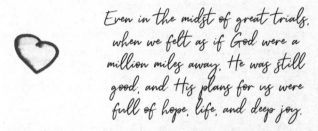

Even in the midst of great trials, when we felt as if God were a million miles away, He was still good, and His plans for us were full of hope, life, and deep joy.

The lie that the Father will abandon us goes back to the garden. When sin entered the world, Adam and Eve were forced to exit the garden. There, the lie of separation—that God is a distant Father who abandons His creation—trickled into the hearts and minds of mankind. It reminds me of the movie *Epic*. My girls love that movie! Every time an arrow from the bad guys hits a tree or a flower, it kills the new growth, and the green life begins to die. The same thing happens to us when we believe lies like, "You're alone and forgotten." We must sing, pray, and meditate on the truth of His love to renew our hearts and minds. God never wanted separation from us. The desire of the triune God has always been to dwell together with us in perfect unity, relationship, and love.

As we look forward from the garden in Genesis, we see that Jesus was the answer to the lie of separation and abandonment. He bankrupted heaven to become the One forsaken by the Father on the cross. He was despised and rejected. He sacrificed all and suffered separation from God so there would no longer be any separation between God and us. Jesus shed His innocent blood and made a way for us to be adopted as sons and daughters (Ps. 27:10). We can stand, confidently knowing

He cannot forget us. He has inscribed us on the palm of His hand (Isa. 49:16). His eyes are always on us (Ps. 34:15).

Going Deeper

You may be under a cloud of depression today, just as Anna was. You may find yourself in a time of hopelessness or intense hardship. Or maybe you have just always viewed God as a distant taskmaster or a disapproving teacher who is waiting for you to mess up.

+ **When you consider who God is, what thoughts come to mind? Is He loving and present, or is He distant and harsh?**

Today slowly contemplate these words from Deuteronomy. Let His presence come and wash over you.

> Be strong and courageous. Do not be afraid or terrified because of them, for the LORD your God goes with you; he will never leave you nor forsake you.
> —DEUTERONOMY 31:6, NIV

+ **What do you sense God's words in this verse saying to you?**

Know that sometimes faith requires speaking and singing the truth over and over before you believe it. My wife and I have a saying that goes, "I'm going to sing it until I believe it!" I leave this as a challenge for you. Don't let your current situation dictate your beliefs concerning the Father's heart. Take hold of the truths in Scripture and make them your anthems of hope. In this place of declaration your mind will be renewed, and you will see who He is and who you are.

Write a declaration that you will speak or sing about your situation. Write your anthem!

WHEN YOU FEEL GOD IS PUNISHING YOU

[God] has indeed no pleasure in afflicting us. He will not keep back
even the most painful chastisement if He can but thereby guide
His beloved child to come home and abide in the beloved Son.
—ANDREW MURRAY

W HEN I WAS a kid, I got spanked and grounded a lot—
and I mean, *a lot* a lot. I think my parents may have
been the official spokespeople for the proverb, "Spare the
rod, spoil the child." (See Proverbs 13:24.) As you've probably
gathered by now, I was the kind of kid who gave them plenty
of opportunities to apply this scripture in my life.

I can remember many days when my mom, completely fed
up, would say, "You wait till your father gets home. He'll deal
with you then." When my mother's mouth ominously issued
those words in her familiar, firm-yet-almost-hushed tone, it
meant only one thing: I was a goner. My dad's spankings
were nothing to trifle with, so the prospect of receiving one
when he returned from work would cause me to be on my best
behavior in hopes of garnering my mother's mercy.

I thought my parents were the meanest, strictest people in
the world. At times I even resented them for their rigidity.
Because I didn't understand the concept of healthy discipline,
I always mistook their correction for malicious austerity. The
severity of their discipline felt like too much for a youngster,
kind of like getting put in the Boo Box in the movie *Hook*.
I didn't realize then that my bad behavior warranted their
actions. If they had sat back and allowed me to break their
rules (and the government's rules at times, for that matter),

it would have been a gross abdication of their responsibility as parents. They knew something I didn't—that their corrections were ultimately for my good.

> My dear child, don't shrug off God's discipline, but don't be crushed by it either. It's the child he loves that he disciplines; the child he embraces, he also corrects.
>
> God is educating you; that's why you must never drop out. He's treating you as dear children. This trouble you're in isn't punishment; it's training, the normal experience of children. Only irresponsible parents leave children to fend for themselves. Would you prefer an irresponsible God? We respect our parents for training and not spoiling us, so why not embrace God's training so we can truly live? While we were children, our parents did what seemed best to them. But God is doing what is best for us, training us to live God's holy best. At the time, discipline isn't much fun. It always feels like it's going against the grain. Later, of course, it pays off handsomely, for it's the well-trained who find themselves mature in their relationship with God.
>
> — HEBREWS 12:6–11, MSG

Proverbs 12:1 says it about as plainly as it can be said: "Whoever loves discipline loves knowledge, but he who hates reproof is stupid." It doesn't get any more clear-cut than that. I don't know about you, but I don't want to be stupid, and the first step toward not being stupid is changing my paradigm concerning God's paternal interjections into my life.

God doesn't correct us for fun. He doesn't discipline us out of anger as some parents do. No, He is the perfect Father from whom all good gifts flow. When the disciples asked Jesus how to pray in Luke 11:2, He responded with, "Our Father in heaven" (NKJV). Note that He didn't say, "High King of Heaven," or even, "Creator of the Universe," but, "Our Father."

Jesus was identifying that at the core of who God is, in the deepest place of His heart, He is Abba, Father. *Abba* is the word that Hebrew children affectionately use to refer to their papas. It's also the word both Jesus and Paul employed to describe their intimate, personal relationships with God. (See Mark 14:36 and Romans 8:5.) This loving Father is the God who corrects us. He doesn't have a mean streak, and He's not coming home stressed out from work, looking for someone to beat. His correction is His mercy. His discipline is His embrace.

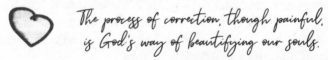

The process of correction, though painful, is God's way of beautifying our souls.

But chastening, as the Scripture says, doesn't usually feel good in the moment. Similar to the way a diamond forms, God's pattern for perfecting us (spiritually speaking) isn't always easy. Intense pressure and extreme heat are the two main ingredients in a diamond's creation, which takes place hidden in the deepest crevices of the earth. But everyone loves diamonds, right? We love to show them off to all our friends and wear them around our necks and wrists. We even wear them in engagement rings to symbolize the magnitude of our love. But no one wants to talk about the process it takes to get them to their final, shiny, beautiful state. We love the finished products after they're harvested from the depths of the earth and meticulously cleaned and cut, but no one wants to talk about raw, untouched diamonds. Why? Because they look like any other rock in the dirt.

The point is, the process of correction, though painful, is God's way of beautifying our souls. The apostle Peter says, "Pure gold put in the fire comes out proved pure; genuine faith put through this suffering comes out proved genuine. When Jesus wraps this all up, it's your faith, not your gold, that God will have on display as evidence of his victory" (1 Pet. 1:6–7, MSG). It isn't about behavioral management; it's about the transformation of the mind and heart through the Father's gentle adjustments.

And that's exactly what they are—adjustments. In the same way that a chiropractor gently adjusts your spine to bring relief, the Father disciplines tenderly. He whispers to our hearts through the Holy Spirit. He doesn't shout angrily or threaten us to motivate us. Small course corrections throughout our lives help us navigate toward the intended final destination of spiritual maturity.

His love is patient and kind. Why? Because we're just as messed up and in need of help as we are delicate. He uses the least severe means to produce the most obedience in our hearts. He unravels us in His love and puts us back together in His grace. When we embrace His discipline, our roots grow deep in the soil of His affection. And deep roots make wonderfully flexible trees.

Going Deeper

When bad things happen, it doesn't mean God is punishing you. Sometimes it just means something bad happened. But when life is hard, you can trust that God is good. He can use even the hardest circumstances and people in your life to

grow you up spiritually. You always have a choice: you [
just react to the discomfort or you can decide how you w
act in response to it. When you choose to respond meekly to
what God allows in your life to purify you, then you come out
shining as pure gold.

♦ **What is going on in your life right now that God may be using
to purify you?**

♦ **How can you respond in submission to God in this situation?**

The situations God is using may seem unfair and even devastating right now. But soon they will be like ashes blown
away in the wind compared to the value of the transformation
God is performing in you through this.

> Therefore we do not lose heart, but though our outer
> man is decaying, yet our inner man is being renewed
> day by day. For momentary, light affliction is pro-
> ducing for us an eternal weight of glory far beyond
> all comparison.
>
> —2 Corinthians 4:16–17

> *Father, strengthen me so I never lose heart when You are
> working on me through people or situations. I give You
> permission to do whatever it takes to make me into the
> person You want me to be.*

N YOU WONDER IF
NG IS ALL YOUR FAULT

think you've blown God's plan for your life, rest in
this. You, my beautiful friend, are not that powerful.
—LISA BEVERE

OR THE PAST few days I've addressed the theme of bad
things happening to God's people. Paul's thorn in the
flesh, Joseph's epic family betrayal, my wife's postpartum
depression—all these things are examples of when life goes
wrong. On Day 16 we looked at the life of Job through the
lens of his self-righteousness, but what if we flip that narrative on its head? Sure, Job may have thought the blessings
in his life were because of his righteous living, but what did
he think when God stripped everything away? What caused
God's "judgments" upon his life?

When God commanded Abraham to bring his only son,
the son whom God promised, to the altar of Mount Moriah,
do you think Abraham may have wondered at least for a split
second what he'd done to deserve such a thing? When bad
things happen to us, it's human nature to believe it's our fault.

Recently I heard a preacher say, "If He wants to use you
greatly, He'll hurt you deeply." While I don't love the obvious
implications of this statement, I resonate deeply with its truth.
The question then becomes, Is God the inflictor of pain, or is
He merely allowing it? And if He's allowing it, why doesn't
He intervene and prevent it? These questions have vast theological ramifications, and scholars land on both sides of the
issue. My personal belief is that sometimes God disturbs us

into our destiny. Sometimes he pushes us out of the nest so we'll spread our wings and fly.

Deuteronomy 32:11 says, "Like an eagle that stirs up its nest, that hovers over its young, He spread His wings and caught them, He carried them on His pinions." At first glance you might be thinking, "What the heck does that mean?" Trust me, I thought the same thing. Then I studied the habits of mother and father eagles, and I found layers of meaning hidden in the words of Moses.

When it's time for the eaglets (the fancy word for baby eagles) to leave the nest and learn to fly, the mother eagle begins to thrash about in the nest, causing great bewilderment and confusion among her young. Frustrated and uncomfortable, the eaglets move to the edge of the nest and begin to test their wings out of sheer desperation. See, discomfort is the mother eagle's intention. She knows that without disruption, her young will remain apathetic in the comfort of the nest. The disruptions to the nest cause the eaglets to learn and develop the skills they need to survive.

Sound like anything you've experienced before? In the moment, the eaglets probably don't understand that what their mom and dad are doing is ultimately for their own good. I imagine they're wondering what they've done to deserve such harsh treatment that is literally putting their lives in danger. They don't know their parents have been training for this moment since before they were born.

When a female eagle is searching for a mate, she does some weird things. One of her mating rituals involves taking a small stick in her talons and flying to about ten thousand feet, at which point she drops the stick. It is then the job of the male eagle courting her to fly down at speeds upwards of one hundred miles per hour to retrieve the stick before it's dashed against the rocks below. The female will do this over and over and with progressively larger sticks until she finds the largest stick (practically a log) that she can carry. If the suitor can perform the task with the giant branch, he gets the girl.

This didn't make sense to me until I realized it's all preparation for the eagles' duties as parents. She is making sure her mate is capable of saving their young when it's time for them to leave the nest. Should one of her babies be unable to fly for itself when pushed out of the nest, she needs to know that her mate can save it before it crashes to its death.

The message of this story is profound: we have a Father who can fly faster than we can fall. Whether the fall is our fault or not, He's able to catch us before we plummet to our sure demise on the rocks of our own choices below. God is so good. He's not like people who write you off if you fall too many times. People give up on you, stop believing in you, and stop giving you second chances. People label you a "hopeless case" if you mess up too many times. But with God we keep getting second chances. He never gives up. He always believes, and He's constantly ready to catch us even if we jump out of the nest prematurely.

We have a Father who can fly faster than we can fall.

Going Deeper

Sometimes you find yourself in the midst of circumstances that are not your fault. It feels as if you're living in a soap opera in which the craziest twists keep happening. But you have a rock to hold on to, your faithful defender who has promised to keep you through all of the struggles.

> In you, LORD, I have taken refuge; let me never be put to shame. In your righteousness, rescue me and deliver me; turn your ear to me and save me. Be my rock of refuge, to which I can always go; give the command to save me, for you are my rock and my fortress.
> —PSALM 71:1–3, NIV

♦ **Which part of this psalm spoke to you the most today? Why?**

Spend a few minutes praying this psalm back to God, allowing Him to be your rock and your fortress in exactly the way you need it today.

MAYBE SOME OF IT
REALLY IS YOUR FAULT

You are not responsible for the bad things that happen to you, but you
are responsible for the patterns you create in response to them. Find
a pattern and you find an opportunity for growth, change, and power.

—HENRY CLOUD

I N YESTERDAY'S DEVOTION we looked at how to respond
when the enemy tries to convince us through our circumstances that everything is our fault. But what do we do
when we face a situation in which we *are* at fault? How do
we take responsibility when our words or actions caused the
sorrow we are experiencing?

I don't know about you, but I find it extremely difficult to
admit when I'm wrong. I'm usually the last to see my faults.
This behavior is rooted in pride—thinking I've got it all together
while everyone else is floundering in befuddlement. Because
of my ego it's very tough for me to genuinely apologize when
I've blown it. But God, in His bulldozing kindness, is always
working to pulverize that self-righteousness right out of me.

It might surprise you, but sorrow over our actions, which
is called "godly sorrow" by the apostle Paul in 2 Corinthians
7:11, can be a gift that leads to a positive, God-honoring
response. Like overgrown grass in the backyard brings out
the lawn mower or a dilapidated room at home sparks a paint
job, sometimes the presence of a problem prompts beautifi-
cation. Crisis is often the spark for innovation. In the same
way, if you are stuck in a destructive cycle, sorrow over your
sin can lead you to repentance, which in turn restores peace

and joy to your life. However, like a long-winded guest who isn't catching the hints that it's time to leave, sorrow tends to overstay its welcome. Unconfronted sorrow can develop into regret, which is a poison to our souls. Its potent venom can be fatal if not dealt with promptly.

Regret, or ungodly sorrow, can fester in the dungeon of our minds when we choose to elevate the gravity of our failure above the power of the Father's forgiveness. This is actually profound arrogance. To believe that our sin is more powerful than His blood is an error of the most grievous kind. Scripture tells us the wages of sin is death. But the good news is, Jesus volunteered to pay the penalty for our sins.

However, even though our punishment is absolved through repentance, sometimes there are natural consequences to our sin. This isn't God's way of angrily exacting His revenge on us. On the contrary, these consequences serve as evidence of the great power of our choices.

When things really *are* your fault (and if you're like me, they often are), repercussions follow. For example, if you are unfaithful to your spouse, God forgives you as soon as you repent. But the natural result of your sin might be broken trust that results in marital difficulty and maybe even divorce. If you are verbally abusive to your children, you can be forgiven immediately through repentance, but emotional and relational damage may linger long past the initial moment of forgiveness.

For me, facing the consequence of my failure is often the most challenging aspect of the healing process. Admitting my faults and forgiving myself is far more difficult than forgiving others. I must continually learn to extend to myself the same grace the Savior does.

But the Lord in His kindness gave me a head start a few

years ago. I was lying on my bed, recapping a message on God's grace I had just given, when I heard the Father say to me, "You want everyone to understand grace so badly, but you, yourself, don't even get it."

As soon as He spoke that phrase, I saw a vivid picture of myself as a teenager slumped over in shame at the foot of my bed. I didn't know exactly why I looked so dejected, but I could tell I was humiliated about something. As I saw this younger version of myself, I couldn't feel compassion, no matter how hard I tried. All I felt was anger and self-hatred.

As I continued to envision my younger self, I saw Jesus walk into my room holding something behind His back. "Oh no! What's that? What's He going to do to me?" I thought. I felt so shameful in His presence that I couldn't even lift my eyes. As I stared down at my feet, to my horror I noticed they were filthy. Then Jesus did the unthinkable—He came close and knelt at my feet. Suddenly it dawned on me that His weapon of choice wasn't a scourge or a whip, as I'd expected, but a bucket of water and a soapy rag. My soul leapt from despair to perfect peace like a bottle rocket on the Fourth of July.

Jesus looked me in the eyes and said, "Will you let Me love you?" My self-hatred made me want to run and hide, but at that moment, for whatever reason, my heart said yes. As Jesus began washing my feet, He said tenderly, "I've forgiven you. Can you forgive yourself?"

Even though the Son of God had condescended to my level and I'd already said yes to Him, my knee-jerk reaction was still to push Him away. I wanted to punish myself. I thought about all the people I had hurt with my words and actions, and it just didn't feel right that I'd be released from my prison while others were still bound in theirs. Jesus then spoke again,

"Will you let Me love you?" This time, I sobbed and nodded my head. As I did, I felt Him take away the anger and self-loathing and replace them with His delight.

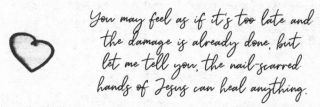

You may feel as if it's too late and the damage is already done, but let me tell you, the nail-scarred hands of Jesus can heal anything.

The Lord often takes me back to that moment. I wish I could say I've never struggled with forgiving myself since then, but I would be lying. In reality it's been a journey of ups and downs. But after all these years I can honestly say I have given the broken pieces of my life to the Father, and in the way that only He can, He's made something beautiful out of them.

Every person on earth, with no exceptions, has sinned and fallen short of the glory of God (Rom. 3:23). Like bombs exploding in public places and sending shrapnel in every direction, our wicked blasts have likely affected or even damaged those close to us: our loved ones, coworkers, friends, acquaintances—and sometimes even strangers.

Maybe you have a marriage or a family relationship that isn't whole and your shortcomings are played continually in your mind like a movie on repeat. Perhaps you've been afraid to confess your sin because you're terrified of the repercussions. In these situations the love of God can become real. Can you forgive yourself with the same forgiveness afforded to you?

Don't continue to punish yourself for a debt Jesus already paid. You're not helping pay the penalty of your sin; you're preventing Him from doing what He wants to do—love you when you least expect it. You may feel as if it's too late and the damage is already done, but let me tell you, the nail-scarred hands of Jesus can heal anything. I've seen Him take the most hopeless situations and turn them into trophies of His grace. I've seen Him sew up the deepest wounds, leaving only tiny scars as eternal reminders that He makes all things beautiful just in time. Don't lose hope. Let Him love you.

Going Deeper

We usually know when we're experiencing the repercussions of our mistakes. Nevertheless, to get out from under the heat, we sometimes try to place blame.

+ Is it hard for you not to assign blame when you find yourself in a mess of your own making? Do you usually blame yourself or others?

+ Instead of blaming anyone, yourself included, what might be a healthier response?

God seems to relish responding to our failures with His unconditional love. He knows that we are sinners, so our mistakes are not a surprise to Him. In fact that's why He came. Paul spoke about the perfection he was striving to reach.

> No, dear brothers and sisters, I have not achieved it, but I focus on this one thing: Forgetting the past and looking forward to what lies ahead, I press on to reach the end of the race and receive the heavenly prize for which God, through Christ Jesus, is calling us.
> —PHILIPPIANS 3:13–14, NLT

+ How can you accept God's forgiveness and forgive yourself as well the next time you blow it?

Day 31

THE POWER OF REPENTANCE

But the prayer of repentance is a refuge for the believer. It is
the godly response of one who knows that he is in sin.
—R. C. Sproul

*T*HE DOCTRINE OF repentance as taught in Scripture is
at the center of the Christian faith. Without it, many
scholars would argue, one cannot be genuinely saved. Repentance is the radical moment of turning back to our Father
after we've run away in sin.

> For godly grief produces a repentance that leads to
> salvation without regret, whereas worldly grief pro-
> duces death. For see what earnestness this godly grief
> has produced in you, but also what eagerness to clear
> yourselves.
> —2 CORINTHIANS 7:10–11, ESV

As Paul said to the Corinthians in the quote above, godly
grief (the conviction of sin) leads to salvation without regret.
The concept is simple: confess your sin and receive forgiveness.
But we can't confuse the simplicity of repentance for weakness. Its depth, both of power and effectiveness, is as deep as
the ocean. Repentance is not primarily a concept to be understood but a truth to be explored personally.

A critical misunderstanding many have when it comes
to repentance is that our sin is merely a behavioral issue.
Therefore our cycle of repentance often looks like the following: commit sin, feel conviction, and repent for our actions.
Conviction and repentance are indeed necessary for living

godly lives, but if we stop there, we ignore the root problems and find ourselves repeating the same sins over and over again as if we are slaves rather than masters.

Concerning these habitual sins, we often remain confused as to why we can't get it right. The reason we sin is not an enigma. In fact it is quite simple. We sin because we have yet to be completely convinced of God's goodness. We don't need a gun pointed to our heads to be led astray. No one sins out of obligation. We sin for one reason: it feels good to our flesh. We don't like the wages of sin, which are spiritual and emotional death, but we certainly enjoy how it feels in the moment.

We know we're breaking God's heart, but we continue indulging, which can cause us to hate ourselves. In our self-loathing, we let the voice of the accuser wield our sin as proof that we are evil (rather than just making bad choices). Then, because God is love and we are "evil," we disqualify ourselves from receiving His forgiveness and acceptance.

This is why encountering God's reckless love is not an option. If we can't receive God's love, we won't enjoy His presence. If we can't enjoy His presence, we'll leave and look for love elsewhere. Living in the light of God's smile is essential in our battle with sin because until we find more satisfaction in the love of God than we do in sin, we will continue to fall. This should be good news!

Psalm 16:11 says God's presence is the only place where there is fullness of joy and pleasures forever (ESV). We have to understand that God made us to experience pleasure. We can't repent away the longing to experience delight because God is the One who put that desire inside us in the first place!

Unfortunately God isn't the only one who knows we were created for pleasure; the enemy has based his entire strategy on this fact. Sin is just a perversion of desires that are meant to be satisfied in God. In Matthew 4 we get a glimpse into Satan's feeble strategy for temptation. He tries to distort Jesus' desires and destiny by telling Him that all the kingdoms of the world would be His if He bowed down and worshiped him (v. 9).

At first glance it seems laughable that Satan could really believe this was a good offer for the Son of God. After all, don't the kingdoms of the world belong to Jesus anyway? But herein lies Satan's only play: a "get out of jail free" card of sorts. He offers Jesus a cross-less path to His destiny. He knows Jesus' inheritance is the nations, so he tries to create a shortcut to His destiny that circumnavigates suffering.

This is precisely the way temptation works in our lives today. But if it's such an easily detected ruse, why do we play the game? Because sin is always readily available. It's like a McDonald's Big Mac or a Hot-N-Ready pizza from Little Caesars—it isn't that good, but boy, does it feel right in the moment. God's way requires waiting. His path requires death to our fleshly desires.

While Satan tells us we are sinners struggling to love God, the Father calls us lovers of God who struggle with sin.

Psalm 145:16 says, "You open your hand and satisfy the desires of every living thing" (NIV). Now you might be thinking, "Wait a second, didn't you just say God's way requires death to my desires? How can God satisfy what He is putting to death?" Simple. Our God is a God of resurrection! Here is the power of repentance: when we acknowledge our wrong-doing and surrender our desires to the Father, we die to the sin and passions that led us down that path. The Father then takes what was previously corrupt and resurrects it in newness and purity. Through repentance, forgiveness, and sanctification, what once was a path to iniquity now leads to life.

It is liberating to know that behind the desire that leads us to sin is actual evidence of God's DNA inside of us. Shame tells us the reason we sin is that our desires, at their core, are completely wicked; therefore there is no hope for us. While Satan tells us we are sinners struggling to love God, the Father calls us lovers of God who struggle with sin. We are the righteousness of Christ! As believers we have hope even in the midst of the most entangling cycles of wrongdoing because we know our sin has an expiration date! A day is coming when we will be fully sanctified and glorified. In that day, sin will be but a faint memory, fading in the blinding light of God's glory and grace.

Sin hangs a veil between God and man; repentance tears it down. It restores the closeness of the relationship that Jesus paid for so dearly. But for us to actually repent, we have to be convinced of His goodness. We can hate sin and its effect on our lives, but for all the agony sin inflicts, it doesn't compare to the pain of feeling rejected by our Father. If there's even an inkling of a belief that God will respond to our sin in anger, we will choose the prison of shame rather than the easy route to restoration. If we think the Father is sitting up in heaven looking down in disgust waiting to unleash all of His anger on us the moment we fall, we won't run to Him. But if we believe the Father is waiting patiently, watching through the windows of heaven to see us walking home on the prodigal road, we will come back to Him every time.

So how do we repent? There's no power in a formula or a meticulously crafted prayer. God is after our hearts. That being said, these three areas should help kick-start you in the right direction.

1. Confess the sin.

Be specific. Remember, God already knows. He's not shocked or disgusted. It's His kindness that is drawing you into His presence so He can forgive you and pour out His love on you!

2. Acknowledge the lie.

Remember, every sin can be traced back to the lie that God isn't good. When we repent, we must uproot these lies by exposing and renouncing them. For example, if you repent for lashing out in anger at a loved one during an intense time of financial stress, don't just say, "I'm sorry for getting angry." Go deeper. Ask the Holy Spirit for revelation about the root issue. Real acknowledgment in this scenario might sound something like this, "Father, I lashed out because I don't trust You with my finances. This stems from the root lie that You aren't good. I renounce that lie, and I ask You to forgive me."

3. Declare the truth.

Repentance isn't paying for half of our sins through penance and letting Jesus' blood foot the rest of the bill. When we repent, we must allow Jesus to take all the punishment for our sin. We tend to resist this grace, but we can combat that by simply receiving the truth about who He says we are. Declare simple yet powerful truths that allow you to receive God's love.

I am chosen.

I am loved.

I am forgiven.

I am the righteousness of God in Christ.

Going Deeper

Perhaps you are used to confessing your sin. You believe 1 John 1:9, which says, "If we confess our sins, He is faithful and righteous to forgive us our sins and to cleanse us from all unrighteousness." Not that it's easy, of course, but it is familiar. However, you may not be used to digging to discover the lie that is behind the sin. It might take some practice, but if you follow the clues, you will be able to expose the lie that has kept you in bondage to that sin for so long.

Bring to mind a sin that you have confessed to God in the last week. Now ask the Holy Spirit to reveal to you the root issue behind this sin. Spend some time pondering and listening.

From the beginning Satan has lied about the character of God, trying to get us to doubt His goodness. Once you recognize the lie on which you have been building your house of sin, give it to God and ask Him to help you replace it with His truth.

• **What are some truths from God's Word that defy the lie from the enemy? Speak them over yourself several times today. Write them down so you can rehearse them this week and break free from habitual sin.**

> *Lord, You are a good God. I believe that and I receive it as truth. I resist any temptation to believe otherwise. Neither my circumstances nor my feelings will convince me to doubt Your goodness again. Thank You for Your kindness toward me.*

CONVICTION VS. CONDEMNATION

To win the war against fear, we must know the true God as He is revealed in the Bible. He works to give us lasting peace. He receives joy, not from condemning us but in rescuing us from the devil. Yes, the Lord will bring conviction to our hearts concerning sin, but it is so He can deliver us from sin's power and consequences. In its place, the Lord works to establish healing, forgiveness, and peace.

—FRANCIS FRANGIPANE

I MAGINE YOU'VE BEEN bedridden for weeks. You decide to see two different doctors to get a diagnosis for the illness from which you are suffering. Plagued by heaviness and discouragement because you know the diagnosis could be grim, you head to your first appointment, determined to get some answers. The first doctor confirms what you've suspected for a while: you are, in fact, quite sick. However, because she can see the big picture of what's going on in your body, she is confident she knows precisely what has caused the sickness and she has the treatment you'll need to recover.

The second doctor also confirms your suspicions that you are very sick. But this doctor tells you he hasn't found the root cause and has no plans to do so. He says it isn't important whether he correctly identifies the cause of the illness, because no matter how aggressively he treats you, it won't go away. He stoically informs you that the problem isn't the sickness itself; it's you. Unfortunately his diagnosis is as hopeless as it is shocking—there's nothing he can do to make you better. According to him, you'll have to learn to live with it.

The first doctor sounds like precisely the kind of person

I'd want caring for me in such a vulnerable time. She took the time to nail the diagnosis with precision and provided the hope and comfort needed to carry on. She created the necessary separation between who the patient is and what is ailing the patient, which provided a sense of optimism concerning the diagnosis. The revelation that the illness would not have the final word provided a surge of strength to carry on, which quickly displaced the sting of the bad news. The second doctor was obviously a quack with whom no one should ever schedule a follow-up appointment (and who should be sued for all he's worth for medical malpractice).

The first doctor represents conviction, and the second represents condemnation. If we ever experienced the above scenario in real life, we'd promptly make the first doctor our primary care physician and would report the other to the board of medicine! Although the decision is overly simplistic in terms of our health care, it's much more complicated when it comes to our spiritual health. However, many of us continue to listen to the voice of condemnation even when it's evident that its diagnoses are always wrong and its opinions are incapable of producing life.

Still, we tend to avoid the voice of conviction because the truth that there might be a problem in us is painful. It's simply human nature to avoid pain at all costs. But as we learned yesterday, we have to repent to stay close to God's heart, and we can't repent without conviction.

Conviction is a loving Father allowing us to feel His pain over the relational separation sin causes in order to draw us back to His heart through repentance.

Condemnation is the archnemesis of conviction. Conviction seeks to liberate us from sin. Condemnation aims to enslave us in it. Have you ever noticed how condemnation counterfeits its spiritual counterpart? Just like a doctor practicing medicine without a medical license, condemnation seeks to undermine God's path to repentance. It emulates aspects of conviction but is powerless to lead you out of sin. Like conviction, condemnation pipes up out of the silence to reveal something overlooked. But its words bring confusion instead of clarity.

Conviction and condemnation have two different authors. Conviction is a loving Father allowing us to feel His pain over the relational separation sin causes in order to draw us back to His heart through repentance. Conversely condemnation is Satan imposing what he feels, which is not quite as warm and fuzzy. He doesn't suggest temporary relational distance but complete and utter separation from the Father.

Conviction and condemnation both employ the same process—opening our eyes to things we couldn't see before and in so doing, allowing us to feel the weight of those things. The critical distinction between the two is that one brings us closer to the Father, and one pushes us further away.

+   Conviction is born from the truth; condemnation germinates in lies.

- Conviction is clean; condemnation is dirty and shameful.
- Conviction says, "There's something wrong with your behavior"; condemnation says, "There's something wrong with you."
- Conviction leads us forward; condemnation keeps us stuck.
- Conviction brings clarity; condemnation brings confusion.
- Conviction lifts our focus to God; condemnation keeps our focus on ourselves.
- Conviction is hopeful; condemnation is hopeless.

If you've experienced the power of repentance that you read about yesterday, you know that conviction is not negative at all. The peace and joy it brings are worth confronting the pain of failure. When you learn the difference between conviction and condemnation, you can freely invite conviction into your life instead of closing yourself off in fear, which leaves you wide open to condemnation's lies.

There is a simple way to discern between conviction and condemnation. If you've repented for a sin yet still feel heavy, confused, or hopeless over it, then you're dealing with condemnation. Once the cross has taken the penalty for your sin, there's no need to exact further punishment upon yourself. It's over. It's done. Anything that tries to get you to punish yourself for something Jesus has already purchased comes from the father of lies and should be renounced and rejected. Romans 8:1 declares that "there is therefore now no condemnation to those who are in Christ Jesus" (NKJV)! Natural consequences may follow our shortcomings, but the penalty and punishment for sin are completely swallowed up in Him. This reality should lead us to a place of incomparable gratitude!

What is the proper response to conviction?

1. Immediate and total repentance.

2. Thanksgiving. It is important to thank Jesus for taking the penalty of our sin and making us whole again. So often we want to punish ourselves in an attempt to prove how truly sorry we are. Stop it! Stop trying to pay for something Jesus paid for! Move on from "woe is me" to "how great is He!"

3. Declaring the truth about who we are. This is probably the most challenging response for many of us because of the chasm between who He says we are and what we feel. It requires faith to believe and receive who He says we are. Every time you repent for something wrong you did, make it a habit to also declare a truth of how loved you are. Here are a few scriptures you can declare over yourself:

   + I am redeemed (1 Cor. 1:30).
   + My sins are forgiven (Eph. 1:7).
   + I am the righteousness of God in Christ (2 Cor. 5:21).
   + I am a child of God (1 John 3:2).
   + Nothing can separate me from God's love (Rom. 8:35–39).

◆   By Jesus' stripes I am healed (1 Pet. 2:24).

Going Deeper

Hebrews 12:1 says that sin sometimes entangles you. Since you know that, you can prepare ahead of time for it. What army would start looking for weapons and ammo after the enemy had attacked them? No, you must prepare your weapons ahead of time—and your most powerful weapon is the Word of God (Eph. 6:17).

◆   **Make a list of three or four sins that have entangled you, that you tend to commit over and over. What is your usual modus operandi when you commit those sins? Write it down so you can examine it.**

Look over the way you handle those sins when you commit them. Do you see any hints of condemnation? As a reminder, condemnation includes feeling dirty and shameful, like there's something wrong with you. It brings confusion and hopelessness, and it keeps your eyes on yourself rather than God.

Now prepare a new battle strategy based on what you've learned today. Write out a new way of dealing with this sin for the next time. You don't have to continue to live with this entangling sin. God will help you get free from it!

FROM GUILT TO GRACE

Haven't you shouldered that guilt long enough?
Let grace happen for heaven's sake.
—Max Lucado

It was told Joab, "Behold, the king is weeping and mourning for Absalom." So the victory that day was turned into mourning for all the people, for the people heard that day, "The king is grieving for his son." And the people stole into the city that day as people steal in who are ashamed when they flee in battle. The king covered his face, and the king cried with a loud voice, "O my son Absalom, O Absalom, my son, my son!" Then Joab came into the house to the king and said, "You have today covered with shame the faces of all your servants, who have this day saved your life and the lives of your sons and your daughters and the lives of your wives and your concubines, because you love those who hate you and hate those who love you. For you have made it clear today that commanders and servants are nothing to you, for today I know that if Absalom were alive and all of us were dead today, then you would be pleased. Now therefore arise, go out and speak kindly to your servants, for I swear by the LORD, if you do not go, not a man will stay with you this night, and this will be worse for you than all the evil that has come upon you from your youth until now." Then the king arose and took his seat in the gate. And the people were all

> told, "Behold, the king is sitting in the gate." And all the people came before the king.
>
> —2 Samuel 19:1–8, ESV

I know that was a long passage of Scripture, but I'm trusting that you read it all the way through (or at least skimmed it meticulously). The life of David is like one big instruction manual on how to flourish (or not flourish) in our seventy years here on earth. So many incredible lessons can be drawn from his achievements and his setbacks. The way David responded after the death of his son Absalom is a beautiful illustration of how we should move from guilt to grace.

In this particular story David and the army of Israel are returning to a recently recaptured Jerusalem after overthrowing David's rebellious son, Absalom. What should have been a time of celebration over their victory became filled with confusion. The troops and people of the land were conflicted; they wanted to rejoice, but David was in deep mourning over the loss of Absalom.

The king wasn't only saddened by the loss of his son (a pain few can understand). He was also wrestling with feeling personally responsible for his death. For two years Absalom stood at the king's gate unchecked, trashing his father's leadership to all of Israel. Instead of confronting Absalom's rebellion like a good father should have, David did nothing. Eventually Absalom's unbridled arrogance grew so great that he rallied an army to overthrow the crown forcibly. What could have been corrected with a simple disciplinary conversation between a father and son turned into a catastrophic loss of life, all because David withdrew into complacency instead of acting like the king and father he was.

David's grief was understandable, and his mourning was justified. But David wasn't just a father; he was still king over all Israel. And the king must carry out his duty not only to his family but to his whole kingdom as well. David had neglected his role as kingly leader, elevating his personal woes over his responsibility to the nation. He was stuck between a rock and a hard place. This is the conundrum into which Joab, the commander over the king's armies, walked. Joab understood David's grief but also had eyes to see that he was slipping into the very thing that led to Absalom's rebellion in the first place—wholesale disengagement.

Before David ever lusted after Bathsheba in his heart, he had first withdrawn as a leader, letting his army go to war while he sat around at home doing nothing. Before Absalom ever usurped the throne, he was fueled by his father's detachment. David's primary issue was not his lust or pride; those were just void-fillers. His main issue was idleness—disengaging from the things God had called him to do. Disengagement often leads to disaster, and for David disaster often occurred under the weight of his inadequacy.

When we focus on our shortcomings and inabilities instead of God's empowering grace, our behavior changes accordingly. Rather than operating from identity, according to whom the Father calls us to be, we get stuck in a cycle of thinking we're not enough, which pushes us further and further away from everyone and everything. Instead of receiving the righteousness of Christ and taking our kingly place at the gate, we hide in our palaces, mourning in shame.

Undoubtedly David's first step forward was not without pain. The city gate was the very location at which Absalom began his coup. To put it plainly, for David to be seated where he belonged, he had to return to the place of his greatest failure.

David didn't have the strength to move from guilt to grace on his own, so God sent Joab. Joab was the one friend who loved David enough to tell him the truth. He said what needed to be said to motivate the mourning psalmist out of his shame and into his identity as king. Proverbs 18:24 says, "There is a friend who sticks closer than a brother." I believe that friend is the Holy Spirit. He's always there to encourage and strengthen, to comfort and guide. All we have to do is ask Him for help. According to Proverbs 27:6, "Faithful are the wounds of a friend." Like Joab the Holy Spirit isn't afraid to give us the hard truth when we need to hear it, even if it hurts. Friendship that isn't honest or convicting isn't friendship at all; it's flattery. A faithful companion is willing to look you in the eyes and tell you when you're off track. A faithful friend will walk with you back to the city gate where you face your guilt and pain head-on.

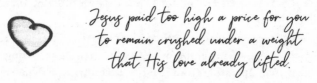

Jesus paid too high a price for you to remain crushed under a weight that His love already lifted.

All the friendship and biblical teaching in the world can't force you to get up out of your depression and back to the seat of unmerited grace. Ultimately you must do it yourself. You might feel as if you'd rather be weeping in the palace alone. You might feel as if you'd rather wallow in shame a little longer. You might even say, "Well, you don't know what happened to me, Cory. You don't know my story." But I do know that Jesus paid too high a price for you to remain crushed under a weight that His love already lifted. It's time to step back into the gate of kingship again. It's who you are. Take your place.

Going Deeper

Some friends will tell you that you have the remnants of lunch on your face and some won't. I prefer the kind who will tell me, and I bet you do too. They are the ones who won't let you stay isolated in the palace, swimming in guilt. They get you out and back into life again. Even if you don't feel as if you have a friend like this, you do have the Holy Spirit, and He is always with you.

+ **Over the last few days you have revisited some sins that have gotten the best of you before. What is something that God has been asking you to do or not do regarding any of these sins?**

Stop right now and ask the Holy Spirit to be your Friend, your Advocate, your Strengthener, your Comforter, and your Helper. Expect in faith that He will actively be all these for you, and lean on Him. Obey whatever God is speaking to you, and He will be more than your best Friend to you.

> And I will ask the Father, and He will give you another Helper (Comforter, Advocate, Intercessor— Counselor, Strengthener, Standby), to be with you forever.
>
> —John 14:16, amp

NOBODY SAID
IT WAS EASY

Day 34

GO AHEAD, ASK HIM THE HARD QUESTIONS

Christians can have doubts and they can have questions, and the unhealthy way to deal with that is to keep them inside where they fester and grow and can undermine our faith. The healthy way to deal with it is to talk about it and be honest about it.

—LEE STROBEL

IN MY THIRTY-THREE years of life I've noticed that most people—especially Christians—are scared of questions. We're afraid to really examine what we know. Maybe it's because we're supremely confident in our knowledge of God. But perhaps, and might I suggest more likely, it's because we're afraid that somewhere along the path of our questioning, we might discover something that shakes our cozy little paradigms to the core. We don't like questions, because we're comfortable and questions have a funny way of stirring up the hornet's nest. It's easier to live with a shallow understanding of Christianity than to wrestle with thoughts that could potentially tangle the covers on the beds of our convenience.

The Bible tells us that God is a mystery. Paul in Ephesians 3:4 refers to the "mystery of Christ." And earlier, in Ephesians 1:9, he talks about the "mystery of His will." In 1 Timothy 3:16 we read, "Great is the mystery of godliness," referring to Jesus' incarnation. Now a mystery is not, as many have misperceived, something completely unknowable, but rather something infinitely knowable. We, as believers, are called to delve into the deep things of God, the mysteries of who He is in all of His beautiful complexity. So how do we get to know Him? Just like we get to know anyone else: we ask questions.

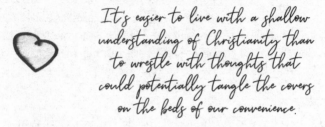

It's easier to live with a shallow understanding of Christianity than to wrestle with thoughts that could potentially tangle the covers on the beds of our convenience.

I've been through lots of difficult circumstances in my life, and I'll tell you that in those seasons, I had lots of questions. Like most people I probably had more questions in trying times than in times of peace. The psalms were my lifeline during those moments. I found solace in the fact that David went through lots of stuff too. And in that stuff, he wasn't afraid to get real with God.

We find the most well-documented of David's displays of brutal honesty before God in Psalm 13. Here's the CASV summary: "How long will You forget me, God? Forever? How long will You hide from me? How long must I wrestle with these anxious thoughts? How long will my enemies make fun of me? Speak to me, or I will die." Pretty intense language, huh? A lot of folks would chalk this up to David's penchant for melodrama and dismiss it. But this was David's vulnerable heart cry before the Father.

Some years ago a trusted leader in my life told me about a practice of his that revolutionized his connection with God. It was something he called a "cuss walk." I remember being offended by the idea at first, thinking, "Wow, sounds disrespectful and irreverent. Don't you know God is holy and should be treated as such?" But as he shared his heart, I began to get it, and this has become a life-changing practice for me as well.

You can give it any name you like, but basically you go into the woods (or whichever solitary place might be at your disposal) and pour out your heart before God in real, raw, incredibly frank honesty—an authentic, no-holds-barred, WWE-battle-royale sort of thing. Anything goes. Nothing is off limits.

For the sake of clarity, the point of this exercise is not to get mad and bring all of your accusations against God. Instead it's to seek understanding of His heart while being transparent about your frustrations. If ever the intent becomes to rail against God for His less-than-perfect dealings without giving Him space to speak in return, you've missed the mark. The goal must always be to comprehend God more honestly and more exhaustively.

I've found that the lens of my circumstance—good, bad, or ugly—is often the greatest magnifier for His goodness. God isn't offended by our questions. He's not thrown off by our anger or frustration. He's waiting to provide the answers we need (although perhaps not the answers we want).

This type of honesty in a human-to-God relationship is unique. Only someone who has experienced God like King David or Paul the apostle can speak with Him as friends do. In contrast consider the way you might behave around someone you don't really know intimately but whom you deeply respect nonetheless. Perhaps you might be a little nervous or maybe overly careful with your words so you don't offend this person. You're probably not going to say everything on your mind. The religious who don't know God for themselves are like this. They say only the things they think He wants to hear so He doesn't get upset with them. But there's no genuine comradery, no authentic closeness. However, when you know Him, you relate as friends do—joyfully, playfully, candidly, unafraid to say something "wrong." Among friends there is honesty, openness, and vulnerability, not secrets and barriers.

So next time you're feeling confused, take solace in this: the mystery of God is just that—a mystery. You don't have to understand everything. In fact I don't think any of us were meant to get it all. Mystery is God's way of cultivating trust in us. It's His way of evening the playing field for all of humanity.

So often we want everything in life to be formulaic (including God). We figure if 1+1=2, then we can act accordingly and never have to encounter anything unexpected. If something's wrong, we look for ten easy steps to make the problem disappear. But God wants us to rely on Him, not on a formula. He wants us to trust Him, to talk to Him when we need help.

Our Western mindsets revolve around control. We want to feel safe. We want to know that everything is going to be OK. But God wants to cultivate confidence inside us that He is a Father who speaks, acts, and injects fresh perspective and revelation into our everyday lives.

Going Deeper

I used to think the various seasons of life, the ups and downs, the trials and triumphs, were about God forcing me to learn tough lessons as a hard-nosed schoolteacher would. Now I realize each season is a loving invitation from a kind Father to dive deeper into His heart of goodness. My prayer lately is, "Break my boxes, God!" I invite you to join me in this request.

One way to break your God boxes is to take an honest walk with God.

◆ **What is something that you'd really like to talk over with God but have been hesitant to bring up with Him? Why have you hesitated?**

Plan sometime today—right now, if you can—to take a walk with God (whether or not you can go anywhere) and bring up the subject you've been wanting to talk with Him about. Pour out your heart as David did, then take time to listen.

This could become a fresh new habit with God, the breaking of an old box that has kept you isolated from Him.

Behold, You desire truth in the inward parts.

—Psalm 51:6, nkjv

Day 35

"FORGIVE US *AS WE FORGIVE*"

In the shadow of my hurt, forgiveness feels like a decision to reward my enemy. *But in the shadow of the cross*, forgiveness is merely a gift from one undeserving soul to another.
—ANDY STANLEY

ORGIVENESS, EEESHHH! I'm going to shoot straight with you: forgiveness is not my favorite topic. I'd much rather talk about grace or sports or the weather or trapezoids or pretty much anything else for that matter! Forgiveness is a formidable topic because it requires fierce bravery. It's a crucial test of whether we've truly received the transformative love of God in our hearts. Love is only real when it's expressed, when it's lived out, right? Well, consider forgiveness the litmus test as to whether you're walking in Jesus' command to "love one another" as He loved us.

The reason forgiveness is such an intimidating topic for many is because it involves opening up old wounds. It is basic human nature to avoid pain at all costs, so intentionally revisiting past wrongdoings can be profoundly agonizing. Jesus never said it would be easy to forgive; He just promised He'd be with us and that He'd help us release those who have sinned against us. We can trust that Jesus is the great physician. If He asks us to open up a wound, it's because He wants to heal it.

Two misunderstandings hold us back from walking in forgiveness. The first is the idea that forgiving someone means excusing and overlooking the offense that person committed—just sweeping under the rug all their misbehavior. This couldn't be further from the truth. God is a God of justice, and His heart breaks over every act of sin that causes someone pain or trauma. Forgiveness doesn't excuse the wrongdoing; it simply stops the poison of its effects from spreading to our hearts. Lewis B. Smedes said it best: "When we forgive, we set a prisoner free and then discover that the prisoner we set free was us."[1]

The second misconception is that forgiving means automatically trusting the offender with the same measure of trust you had before the offense. Again, this is not the truth. Sometimes forgiveness clears the rubble and debris from the floor of the relationship so a new foundation can be built, but forgiveness does not equal trust. Forgiveness affects the past, while trust deals with the future. Forgiveness doesn't require us to rebuild relationship where trust was broken. Often, especially in the case of a repeated offense or in situations where the offender is unrepentant, forgiveness without restored trust is actually best for future healing. Healthy boundaries are important.

I think true forgiveness is the greatest testament to the power of the reckless love of God. In Matthew 18 (probably the most famous chapter in Scripture concerning forgiveness and reconciliation) Peter asks Jesus how many times he should forgive his "brother or sister" who sins against him. He asks, "Up to seven times?" (v. 21, NIV). I imagine he felt noble for suggesting such a "big" number.

But Jesus' answer probably caused him to recoil in embarrassment. "I tell you, not seven times, but seventy-seven times" (v. 22, NIV).

Peter's inner response was imaginably something like, "What?! Are you kidding me? How could you ask me to let someone hurt me seventy-seven times?! That's…(wait for it) reckless!" It might seem as if Jesus was suggesting that Peter allow people to trample him underfoot, to take advantage of him, to slap him in the face—and I think that's precisely what He was doing.

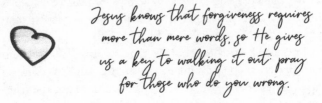

Jesus knows that forgiveness requires more than mere words, so He gives us a key to walking it out: pray for those who do you wrong.

In Matthew 5:38–40 (NIV) Jesus says, "You've heard that it was said, 'Eye for eye, and tooth for tooth.' But I tell you, do not resist an evil person. If anyone slaps you on the right cheek, turn to them the other cheek also. And if anyone wants to sue you and take your shirt, hand over your coat as well." Again, WHAT?! In a culture that tells us to fight for ourselves, to stand up for our rights, and to crush anyone who disagrees with us, Jesus' teaching sounds ridiculous, even silly. It just doesn't make any sense. To forgive is to be seen as weak, maybe even as a pushover or someone to be taken advantage of. But that is the command, nonetheless.

Jesus exemplified the power and grace of true forgiveness on the cross. He was able to look at the very people who crucified Him and ask the Father to forgive them. Like the good teacher Jesus is, He provides both the clear command and the grace to walk it out. Matthew 5 also says, "You have heard that it was said, 'Love your neighbor and hate your enemy.' But I tell you, love your enemies and pray for those who persecute you, that you may be children of your Father in heaven. He causes his sun to rise on the evil and the good, and sends rain on the righteous and the unrighteous. If you love only those who love you, what reward will you get?" (vv. 43–46,

NIV). Jesus knows that forgiveness requires more than mere words, so He gives us a key to walking it out: pray for those who do you wrong.

A while back a close friend of mine hurt me deeply. Time went by, and I found myself spending a lot of time thinking about this person and how much I hated him. I knew I was in a prison of unforgiveness, but when I tried to give it to the Father through confession, I still felt hatred and anger toward the offense and the offender alike. I remember saying to God, "I've tried so many times to forgive, but I still hate this person whom You love." I heard the Lord reply, "Have you prayed for him?"

At first, I wanted to pray something like, "Dear God, I pray for _____, that You would show him how stupid he is. Make his life a living hell until he comes crawling back to me, begging for mercy. AMEN!" At that moment, as I struggled to muster a heartfelt prayer, I realized that saying, "I forgive you," while still harboring animosity in my soul had been easier than I imagined. But I also found it nearly impossible to pray an authentic prayer of blessing over someone and not genuinely begin to love him.

For several weeks, whenever I thought of this individual, I said a ten-second prayer of blessing for him. I didn't pray a prayer of imprecation as I had wanted to the first time. Instead I prayed that God would pour His love and favor over his life. Over time I noticed that when I thought of this person, instead of anger and rage, I started having compassion toward him.

Eventually I was able to release completely the hatred I was shouldering. I was able to separate the wrongdoing from the wrongdoer and see him through Jesus' eyes—the same eyes that looked down from the cross at the ones mocking Him and saw more than their sin. Jesus saw their hearts and decided to love them even though they didn't deserve it. I realized Jesus wasn't ready to condemn the person who hurt me, so neither was I. What a beautiful way to show the Father that we've let His reckless love sink deep into our hearts.

Going Deeper

The apostle John talks about who Jesus was and why He came into the world.

> The true light that gives light to everyone was coming into the world. He was in the world, and though the world was made through him, the world did not recognize him. He came to that which was his own, but his own did not receive him.
>
> —John 1:10–11, NIV

I don't believe anyone can receive more rejection than Jesus did. He came to the very world that was made through Him, yet those who were His own did not recognize or receive Him. Given that, nothing reveals His reckless love more than these words that He spoke from the cross:

> Father, forgive them, for they do not know what they are doing.
>
> —Luke 23:34, NIV

Admittedly we have some big shoes to step into if we want to follow Jesus in forgiveness. But it's a command, not a suggestion. And it's for our own good.

Ask Jesus for His heart toward the person against whom you hold unforgiveness. Forgive as an act of faith. Then pray for that person by faith. Pray what you would want someone to pray for you. Continue to pray, day after day, until Jesus' heart of reckless love is formed in you.

Day 36

TURNING THE HEARTS OF FATHERS AND SONS

Jesus speaks as if we are all brokenhearted. We
would do well to trust His perspective on this.
—JOHN ELDREDGE

As I write this, I'm staring out the second-story window
of my downtown loft into yet another cold, rainy
October day in Michigan (when all I wanted today was some
sunshine). I am, for what feels like the trillionth time, halted
by a blank page that seems to taunt me like an overconfident,
swaggering boxer, unfazed by my piddling blows and signaling
for more. It is Muhammad Ali, and I am an ant. See, I've tried
countless times to write this devotion only to fail so wretchedly
that I'm forced to delete everything and start again, with that
familiar blank page hurling its insults anew. While this is only
Day 36 of 40, I saved this bit of writing for last. And I guess it's
fitting because it's probably the most daunting and intimidating
in terms of subject matter.

Wounds from our fathers and mothers, I believe, are the
deepest of all. Maybe that's because our parents were the very
ones given to us to instill a sense of belonging and identity, so
when they miss the mark even in the most infinitesimal of ways,
it's especially painful. Fathers and mothers call us forth into
our destinies. They bestow upon us an inheritance when it's
time for them to leave. They are, in many ways, our windows
into heaven, showing us who and what the One on the throne
is really like. But when those windows become tainted or tar-
nished, oh, how our imaginations run wild. We fancy God as

an abuser, a tyrant, or maybe worst of all, a ghost—His ethereal shadow haunting us instead of holding us.

My father was a harsh man, beleaguered by the stress and worry of caring for a family of four. Abusive tirades were a normal part of my childhood, and their effects were something I quickly learned to stuff down so deep I thought I'd never have to reckon with them. But I've learned that suppressed feelings eventually give way to hard hearts.

I can remember one incident in particular that marked my days as a young man. I was around twelve years old, just entering adolescence and plagued by the questions surrounding such a rite of passage. My dad and I were chopping wood outside our house in North Carolina. At just five feet tall and ninety pounds, I found that the ax made for a full-grown man was far too heavy for me. I was working on a large stump and floundering about miserably. I remember looking up at my dad, hoping he'd step in and offer a helping hand or a word of encouragement, but no such thing happened. Instead he glared at me with a look of such disgust that I thought he must have mistaken me for someone (or something) else. The words he spoke in that moment scarred me for many years afterward. "You're pathetic. Just give me the ax and get out of my sight." I was crushed. All I wanted was for him to help me, to affirm me in my weakness. I wanted him to kneel down, look me in the eyes and say, "It's OK, son. I'll teach you," and grab my hand and show me how real men cut wood.

In the years since this incident, I've often revisited it in my mind, asking the Father where He was in all of it. His answer has always been the same. "I was right there...with both of you. You needed Me to lift the weight of the ax and he needed Me to lift the weight of the world." I still weep at

His response. So tender. So loving. So measured. He didn't take sides and neither do I.

My dad and I have since spoken at length about the fissures and cracks in the foundation of our relationship, and although it's not perfect by any means, we have worked to repair it and now stand on solid footing. The keys to reconciliation were honesty, hard conversations, and genuine repentance (not to mention lots and lots of tears).

Today's reading focuses on turning the hearts of fathers to sons, and sons to fathers—no easy task. In fact I believe one of the enemy's greatest strategies in keeping us far from God is building walls and barriers between parents and children (and like me many of us find ourselves in both groups).

Let's turn to the text in Malachi 4:6 to take a closer look. "And he will turn the hearts of the fathers to the children, and the hearts of the children to the fathers, lest I come and strike the land with a curse" (NKJV). First it's interesting to note that this is the final verse in the Old Testament. It's as if God is declaring to His people, "I will yet heal your image of who I am, and I will do it through My Son!" The very next word from Scripture is Jesus' genealogy and birth.

I believe one of the enemy's greatest strategies in keeping us far from God is building walls and barriers between parents and children.

While God didn't personally put the canon and its chronology together with His own hands, I believe the Holy Spirit orchestrated it all strategically. Jesus is the image of the Father, unraveling the riddle of human existence. He makes sense of what it means to be alive, to be a son. He shows us what it's like to live in perfect unity with the Father. He is the ultimate blueprint for us as sons and daughters.

In John 15:15 Jesus declares, "I no longer call you servants, because a servant does not know his master's business. Instead, I call you friends, for everything I have learned from my Father I have made known to you" (NIV).

Jesus' words ring just as true in regard to discipleship as parenting. How many of us have tried to be friends with our eight-year-olds? We end up doing things parents just should not do (or allow) in the name of being a cool mom or dad. Playing video games and eating junk food until 1:00 a.m. on a school night probably isn't the best practice. Nor is jumping off the roof onto a dilapidated trampoline two stories below. Yet we do silly things like these to gain our kids' approval, thinking that being their friends is the end goal. But are we trying to meet a need inside of ourselves that shouldn't be met through our children?

I believe it's really not until our kids mature and become adults that we can truly be friends with them. Then the boundaries that were necessary for them as little children are replaced with trust and freedom. Jesus led His disciples like little children for a time before they were seasoned enough for the "training wheels" to be removed. When they were ready, He graduated them from servanthood into sonship, revealing what He was doing and why. Identity is the distinction between slavery and sonship. A servant doesn't care about his master's house; a son cares about his father's house because his inheritance is wrapped up in it.

The second thing of note to me is the fact that "He will turn the hearts of the fathers to the children" comes before the "children to the fathers." Fathers and mothers are the ones who must go first in seeking restoration. They're the ones who must take initiative to pursue their wounded sons and daughters. The buck stops (or perhaps more accurately starts) with them.

When children rebel (as they often do), fathers and mothers can perceive that as a form of rejection and in turn close off certain parts of their hearts to avoid pain. But parents still have the responsibility to pursue their children even when it hurts. It's simply their job because it's the example our Father in heaven set. Being pushed away isn't permission to stop pursuing. Parents must keep chasing after the hearts of their children no matter what, because if a child's rebellion causes his or her parents to turn away in self-preservation, the child will feel unvalued and uncared for, which will only perpetuate the cycle of toxicity.

I believe repentance is the key to turn hearts, and I believe it starts with fathers and mothers. I've seen this in my own life countless times. When I blow it with my son and actually own the wrong by apologizing and repenting to him, the rift between us is closed, leaving zero space or time for it to expand. All it takes is me humbling myself and admitting that I messed up (which is easier said than done). We as parents don't want to admit that we're weak and broken, especially to our kids. We'd rather keep them "safe" in the illusion that we're Superman or Wonder Woman. But the truth is, when we confess our faults to our kids, it's the healthiest, most "superhuman" thing we can do, and God honors it. Breakthrough in our relationships with our kids is often found on the altar of surrender and repentance.

The final line, "Lest I come and smite the land with a curse," is critical too. I believe the curse God is referring to here is simply the natural result of the great chasm between the hearts of parents and children—an orphan spirit. This gap is where fatherlessness festers. I believe we are seeing the effects of this epidemic run rampant in our day. The nonexistence of healthy relationships actually propagates the problem.

We, as believers, are called to carry a spirit of adoption by which we cry out, "Abba, Father!" But many of us, because of a lack of identity (which is often the result of unresolved relational issues), get stuck in an orphan spirit, which is only healed when we open our hearts to the love of God. And sometimes opening our hearts to the love of God looks like opening our hearts to the ones around us. We are found by a Father but formed in a family. Perhaps surrounding ourselves with healthy community is the first step on the road to healing.

Going Deeper

I know this is a serious devotion today. We have talked about the issues that both parents and children can have because of broken relationships between them. I don't know whether you are a parent or a child or, like me, both. Or perhaps you are dealing not only with pain concerning your biological parents but also your caregivers—those who raised you. Maybe the idea of having an orphan spirit hit you to your very marrow. Or you might be one of those adult children wishing your parents would reach out to you and begin the healing. No matter which scenario you identified with, a beginning is needed.

During another time of attempted restoration, the Jewish exiles had returned from Babylon to Jerusalem. Zerubbabel was leading the effort to rebuild the temple of God, but opposition caused a long delay. The Lord, through Zechariah, encouraged the work to continue, promising, "Zerubbabel is the one who laid the foundation of this Temple, and he will complete it" (Zech. 4:9, NLT). Then the Lord added, "Do not despise these small beginnings, for the LORD rejoices to see the work begin (v. 10).

First we see the encouragement that the work that needs to be done and the foundation will both be accomplished. Then the Lord praises even small steps toward its completion.

+ **Is there any small beginning that you can take this week to work on the foundation of your relationship with your children? Your parents? Your caregivers?**

The first step is the biggest step, and the Lord "rejoices to see the work begin," no matter how small the first step is. Ask the Lord to help you and fill you with courage right now, then make your move.

RUN BACK TO THE FATHER

I am the prodigal son every time I search for unconditional love where it cannot be found.
—HENRI NOUWEN

OST CHRISTIANS ARE familiar with the story of
the prodigal son. In fact we know it so well that we
have practically redefined the word *prodigal* in our "Chris-
tianese" lexicon. If you ask the average believer what it means,
they'll tell you something like, "Evil, backslidden, ungodly, or
runaway." But the correct definition of *prodigal* is "spending
money or resources freely and recklessly; wastefully extravagant."[1] It also means "having or giving something on a lavish
scale."[2] I would argue that these definitions are not neces-
sarily innately negative. They could just as easily be ascribed
to the father as the son in the story.

We all know how the parable goes. The irresponsible son
demands his inheritance from the father and promptly goes
off and spends it all on lavish living. Was this a wise move
on the son's part? Absolutely not, but it wasn't heinous either.
Most young people I know make tons of poor decisions—
usually out of a lack of maturity rather than malicious intent.
The point is, the prodigal son gets a bad rap when what he did
wasn't exactly murder in the first degree, as most Christians
tend to perceive.

I think we look at the prodigal son with such disdain
because at the beginning of his story he's one of the "bad guys"
of the Bible. We want to cast blame on someone, and he happens to be readily available. He becomes the scapegoat for all

of our sins and wrongdoing. He makes us feel better about ourselves. Even though his "crime" isn't deserving of the death sentence heaped upon him, many readers cast their stones nonetheless.

But I suggest that the son's tragic downfall doesn't fit the hate he receives. Perhaps it was nothing more than a miscalculation—a massive miscalculation to be sure, but a miscalculation nonetheless. The prodigal son got it wrong somewhere along the way, and when he figured it out, like many of us, he considered himself too far gone to come home.

I imagine the shame he must've felt waking up in a pigpen one morning—no money, no friends, and everyone he thought cared about him having absconded in the dead of night when they realized he didn't have the means to entertain them anymore with his extravagant parties. With the buzz from the night before finally wearing off, he realizes he's left with nothing but his guilty conscience. At rock bottom he comes to his senses. "How many of my father's hired servants have food to spare, and here I am starving to death!" he says to himself. "I will set out and go back to my father and say to him: 'Father, I have sinned against heaven and against you. I am no longer worthy to be called your son; make me like one of your hired servants'" (Luke 15:17–19, NIV).

He didn't even dare to consider himself a son anymore. He believed his foolish actions had disqualified him from being part of the family. I imagine him on the long walk home, rehearsing the words he'd say to his father over and over again, trying to perfect them, trying to find a way to earn back his place in the family. He was undoubtedly expecting his father to be angry and tell him to get lost and never come back.

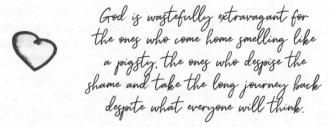

God is wastefully extravagant for the ones who come home smelling like a pigsty, the ones who despise the shame and take the long journey back despite what everyone will think.

But to his surprise, while he was yet a long way off, his father comes running. Filled with compassion, his father throws his arms around the son, kissing his neck with paternal affection. In Middle Eastern culture it was shameful and foolish for a man to gird his loins (which means he pulled up his pants really high) and run because it violated widely accepted social norms. But the father, seeing his lost son in the distance, couldn't have cared less about social norms. He abandoned all semblance of religious piety for the sake of love—not because he wanted to make a theological statement, but because embracing his son was supremely important. That's the love of God.

I like the way Timothy Keller explains it in his book *The Prodigal God*: "In this story the father represents the Heavenly Father Jesus knew so well….Jesus is showing us the God of Great Expenditure, who is nothing if not prodigal toward us, his children. God's reckless grace is our greatest hope, a life-changing experience."[3]

Our prodigal God kills the fatted calf and throws a feast for sinners when they deserve to starve. He is wastefully extravagant for the ones who come home smelling like a pigsty, the ones who despise the shame and take the long journey back, despite what everyone will think. When any of us says, "I'm no longer worthy of being called Your child," He says, "Quick! Bring the best robe, ring, and sandals! For this child of mine was dead and is alive again! My child was lost but now is found!"

Going Deeper

Perhaps you've never looked at the story of the prodigal son this way. Maybe you never knew what *prodigal* really meant until you read this, and you surely would not have applied that word to the father in the story. Either way, what is most important is getting a fresh revelation of the Father's extravagant—and prodigal—love.

+ Have you ever thought of the Father's love as just as reckless as the son's spending habits? How does seeing it that way affect you?

+ How do you need or want the Father's love to be extravagant and reckless toward you today, right now?

Go to Him just as you are and blurt it all out to Him. Tell Him of your need as the son did with the father in this story. God's response to you will not be less lavish than His response to the prodigal son.

GO FORWARD IN THE HEART OF GOD

There are far, far better things ahead than any we leave behind.
—C. S. LEWIS

*J*EREMIAH 29:11 HAS been used (and overused) on everything from graduation cards to cheesy inspirational Instagram art. We've heard this verse so many times, we tend to glaze over it, remaining mostly unaffected by its truth and power. Unfortunately, when words are handled too often, they dwindle in value. Like a blade dulled from overuse, words become blunt from repetition. But the Word of God never loses its edge. If we'll let it have its way, it is sharper than any two-edged sword. So let's take this moment and let this verse speak to us and pierce us to the core.

> For I know the thoughts that I think toward you, says the LORD, thoughts of peace and not of evil, to give you a future and a hope.
>
> —JEREMIAH 29:11, NKJV

Right now, in this very moment, the Father is excitedly pondering the way He is going to lead you into a great and glorious future. He's dreaming about all the good and perfect gifts He's going to give you. His thoughts are wild with color concerning all the ways He wants to reveal Himself to you, from monumental moments like the birth of a child to seemingly normal moments such as singing to Him and feeling His love in return. The future is bright for those who know the character and nature of the One who holds it.

And wait, there's more good news! God has written an

incredible story of victory for your life, and no force in creation is powerful enough to stop Him (or you) from bringing it to completion. Paul says in Romans 8:38–39 (ESV), "For I am sure that neither death nor life, nor angels nor rulers, nor things present nor things to come, nor powers, nor height nor depth, nor anything else in all creation, will be able to separate us from the love of God in Christ Jesus our Lord." Not only is your future so bright, you'll have to wear shades (sorry, I had to), but there's nothing that can rob you of it.

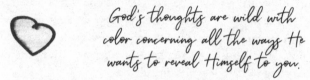

God's thoughts are wild with color concerning all the ways He wants to reveal Himself to you.

God's plan for you is like an all-inclusive, all-expenses-paid trip to your dream destination. I'm not talking about those trips that appear to be free but end up costing you an arm and a leg in hidden fees (not to mention having to spend half your days stuck in a room with a pushy salesman trying to coerce you into buying a time-share). I'm talking about the kind of trip where everything has already been purchased and given to you for real (I mean, *for real* for real). It's an entirely unmerited gift—one too good to be true. Your airline ticket, hotel, food, spa days, ride to the airport, and gratuities are covered. Sounds pretty fantastic, huh? With everything booked in advance, the only thing that can prevent you from taking advantage of this once-in-a-lifetime opportunity is choosing not to get in the car sent to take you to the airport. The path is laid out; all you have to do is choose to accept.

To state the blatantly obvious, our future with God isn't exactly a vacation. Comfy, carefree times are ahead for sure, but so are trials and tribulations galore. Moving forward always means courageously facing obstacles such as fear, doubt, pain, and persecution. But in John 16:33 (ESV) Jesus says, "In the world you will have tribulation. But take heart; I have overcome the world." Notice that Jesus doesn't say, "I am going to overcome the world." His statement is past tense; He has already done it.

This isn't merely a spiritual concept with zero personal application in our lives. Jesus has already overcome every future difficulty yet to be faced. Let me put it this way: for every future hardship you will face, there are millions of potentially victorious outcomes for which Jesus has already paved the way. Your job isn't to overcome in your own strength; it's just to cling to the One who already has.

When it comes to moving forward, no one has inspired me more than King David (as if we haven't talked about him enough). No matter how many times he fell, he got right back up. He never let his failure define him or slow him down in his reckless pursuit of the Father's heart. Unlike the prodigal son David never delayed his trip back to the Father's house. When convicted, the psalmist quickly repented. He didn't blame anyone else, he didn't downplay his sin, and he didn't go through religious motions. He owned it, confessed it directly to God, and then got back up and received all the favor he knew was still available for his life. How did he do both repentance and restoration so well? He knew the secret: God never denies a broken and contrite heart. A fully repentant and vulnerable heart is irresistible to the Father.

So, when facing the future, we need to come to terms with the fact that even in our best efforts, we are going to fail. We must resolve that no matter how many times we fall, we're going to get back up again.

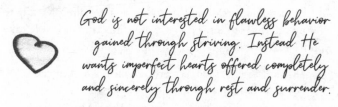

God is not interested in flawless behavior gained through striving. Instead He wants imperfect hearts offered completely and sincerely through rest and surrender.

My story is not one of perfection by any means. I'm sure you're wise enough to know the "'Reckless Love' guy" doesn't walk in sinless perfection. But I can promise you that for every victorious word I've written in this book, I could write a thousand on my mess ups. Somewhere along the journey I learned the secret that earned David the right to be called a man after God's own heart. God is not interested in flawless behavior gained through striving. Instead He wants imperfect hearts offered completely and sincerely through rest and surrender. Proverbs 24:16 (NIV) says, "For though the righteous fall seven times, they rise again." Being righteous isn't about never falling; it's about having reckless confidence in the heart of a good Father to move forward afterward.

No matter how epic your future shortcomings might be, the car will still be waiting in your driveway, ready to whisk you away to the glorious future that Jesus bought for you in blood. Your sin doesn't cancel the trip. His thoughts toward you haven't changed. They're still brimming with hope concerning the future He has planned for you. The gifts of repentance and forgiveness are always readily available the moment you fall— and so is His love. Nothing can separate you from Him. So, with buoyant hearts, let us take our first steps toward the triumphant tomorrows God has in store for us.

Going Deeper

Maybe as you are reading this today, you are almost ready to give up on God's grace. I mean, how many times can He take you back after failing? Well, an infinite number of times!

> My sacrifice, O God, is a broken spirit; a broken and contrite heart you, God, will not despise.
>
> —PSALM 51:17, NIV

+ **What do you feel that God cannot forgive you for one more time?**

The moment the Holy Spirit convicts us of sin is the moment when His grace is present to forgive. He longs to restore you back into perfect relationship with Him.

Right now, no matter whether you feel like it or not, ask God to forgive you and restore you. Then thank Him for the bright future He has for you, no matter what your past was like.

> *Father, I thank You that You are a forgiving God. You have been so, so kind to me. Now set my feet along Your path to Your glorious future for me. I know that we can do this together and that You will be with me every step of the way. I choose today to move forward with a giant smile on my face because You are compassionate and You are guiding me every moment. Amen.*

> In repentance and rest is your salvation, in quietness and trust is your strength.
>
> —ISAIAH 30:15, NIV

SECTION V

ANSWERING
THE CALL

READY TO ENCOUNTER
GOD'S RECKLESS LOVE

Whenever God reveals His nature in a new way, it is always for a purpose. He created you for a love relationship with Him. When He encounters you, He is allowing you to know Him by experience. Encounters with God are always an expression of God's love for you.

—HENRY T. BLACKABY

HAVE YOU EVER finished reading a book and felt a profound sense of accomplishment? When I was in grade school, my mom put my sister and me in the "Book It" program. Every time we finished reading a book, we would get to take a trip to—you guessed it—the illustrious Pizza Hut! There we would receive and subsequently demolish our free personal pan pizzas! As I dove into the next book, my ten-year-old self could practically taste the cheesy goodness that would soon be mine. I was often guilty of skimming through the last few chapters, perhaps to my own detriment, to receive my tasty prize sooner.

I doubt that anyone is buying you pizza after you finish the final words of this book. (Although that would be nice, wouldn't it?) Still, I'd like to challenge you to ask yourself what you're walking away with as you near completion. Even now take a moment to ponder what you have received thus far.

The driving motivator for me in writing this devotional was simple: I wanted to provide an on-ramp for you to encounter the love of God in a new and authentic way. That's it. I wasn't trying to impress you with my expansive knowledge, and I certainly didn't intend to arm you with a bunch of Bible facts to use against people with whom you disagree. I simply desired to bring you into the story of my life to show you how fiercely personal and how great His reckless love is for us. I hope that as you've read the various stories and illustrations throughout our forty-day journey, you've gained new and greater understanding of who God is and what He's like.

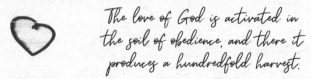

The love of God is activated in the soil of obedience, and there it produces a hundredfold harvest.

But if the words only enter your head without making the eighteen-inch journey to your heart, reading this book will be like purchasing fruit and vegetable seeds for your garden but never actually planting them in your soil. Technically you possess the ability to produce a crop, but since an unplanted seed can never grow, it will never produce fruit. The DNA that carries all the potential for life inside a seed lays dormant unless it is planted in the ground. Similarly, if we only assent to the love of God with our minds, we will walk around with truths in the form of seed packets. The Word has to mature and grow to the point of producing life and sustenance for our souls. For God's love to bring forth fruit, it has to be received by a fully surrendered heart. Over the years I have come to understand that the love of God is activated in the soil of obedience, and there it produces a hundredfold harvest.

In Ephesians Paul uses the language of seed and harvest when referring to God's love as something so strong that it has the power to root and ground us. Paul prays that God "may grant you to be strengthened with power through his Spirit in your inner being...that you, being *rooted* and *grounded* in love, may have strength to comprehend with all the saints what is the breadth and length and height and depth, and to know the love of Christ that surpasses knowledge" (Eph. 3:16–19, esv, emphasis added).

Paul begins his prayer by asking God to strengthen His church so the seed of love can grow. He is praying that we would be deeply grounded in the knowledge of God's love. We may think, "That sounds great! I'll take some of that supernatural strength!" as if it were a spontaneous deposit that hits our bank accounts effortlessly and suddenly. However, the Greek word here for *strengthen* comes from the word *kratos*, which implies something altogether more strenuous and involved.[1] In the original language it denoted a tearing of a muscle so that it might be rebuilt.

Our spirits are not all that different from our natural muscles. A literal tearing away must come before a rebuilding of strength. Tearing is painful, so sometimes it seems easier to let the truth stay put in our minds and never plant it in our hearts. But our response proves whether we have genuinely received and planted the love of God. Obedience to the Word is the soil that will cause the seed to flourish.

The truths you've (hopefully) received from this forty-day journey will only strengthen you if you open your heart and let God's love find you right where you are. I encourage you to ask God to tear away the false mindsets and allow His truth to rebuild something far stronger than what previously existed. Being confronted with areas of our lives that we haven't surrendered to Jesus can be painful, but if we receive the invitation, the pain will turn to gain (to use the tired old cliché). The tearing is never arbitrary with God. He only tears what He intends to strengthen.

So, are you ready to encounter God's reckless love? My earnest desire is that through reading about moments when God revealed His kindness to me, you have seen striking similarities with how the Father is making Himself known to you. My story is unique for sure, but it isn't exclusive or elitist. Your journey might take a different path from mine, but we will all end up at the same destination. God's reckless love finds us broken and ineligible; yet there He pulls up a seat for us when we least deserve it.

Going Deeper

Being a Christian is all about the heart. That's where the seeds of the Word are planted, and that's where obedience begins. Jesus had a lot to say about the heart.

> Our words come from the overflow of our hearts (Matt. 12:34).
>
> Our hearts will follow our treasure (Matt. 6:21).
>
> The evil one snatches seed from our hearts so it won't bear fruit (Matt. 13:19).
>
> We can talk to God but be far from Him in our hearts (Mark 7:6).
>
> We can doubt in our hearts and negate our faith (Mark 11:23).
>
> Out of our hearts come evil thoughts (Matt. 15:19).
>
> We ponder and reason in our hearts (Luke 2:19; 9:47).
>
> Our hearts can become hardened (Matt. 19:18).

Our hearts can be troubled, afraid, and full of sorrow, but they can also rejoice (John 14:27; 16:6, 22).

Our hearts can be weighed down with partying and the worries of life (Luke 21:34).

Rivers of living water (the Holy Spirit) can flow out of our hearts (Luke 7:38–39).

Our hearts can be cheerful and courageous because Jesus has overcome the world (John 16:33).

We are to love God will all our hearts (Matt. 22:37).

Our hearts can be good soil that receives the Word and bears fruit (Luke 8:15).

+ **Which of these truths about the heart meant the most to you today? Why?**

+ **What heart adjustment do you need to make today to have a fully surrendered and obedient heart?**

> *Lord, I surrender my heart to You as fully as I know how today. Strengthen me so that my heart rejoices with obedience to Your Word. I want to bear good fruit for You. Amen.*

THE SMILE OF GOD

Learn much of the Lord Jesus. For every look at yourself, take ten looks at Christ. He is altogether lovely....Live much in the smiles of God. Bask in his beams. Feel his all-seeing eye settled on you in love, and repose in his almighty arms.
—Robert Murray M'Cheyne

ABOUT A YEAR before "Reckless Love" was written, Anna and I took part in what I would now call one of the most important and pivotal events of our lives: a couples retreat at the Helser farm in Sophia, North Carolina. If you're not familiar with Jonathan and Melissa Helser, their songs might ring a bell or two. "No Longer Slaves" and "Raise a Hallelujah" are just a couple of their many masterpieces that have touched the world. They are two of the most fiercely loving, kind, and vulnerable people I know. Their lives and ministries have helped Anna and me in ways words could never express, and those five days spent at their farm in the early summer of 2016 were nothing short of life changing. I believe they were, in some ways, directly responsible for the birth of the song "Reckless Love."

Jonathan (Jonny for short) has a unique understanding of and a closeness to the heart of the Father like no one I've seen before. He's the type of guy who can unashamedly call God "Papa" and make everyone in the room cry like a baby at his tenderness and authenticity. He carries the kind of glow only a man who regularly spends time with God face-to-face possesses—the type of brightness I imagine Moses had on his face after coming down from Mount Sinai with the two tablets. His relationship with "Papa" is enough to provoke jealousy in the heart of even the most ardent believer. The thing Jonny loves to talk about more than anything is the smile of God—and unironically, his words are always spoken (or should I say squeezed) through a grin so wide it seems to span from the northern mountains of California to the crystalline sands of Florida's coast.

One afternoon toward the beginning of the retreat, after hearing Jonny talk about the face of God and the smile of the Father hundreds of times already, I decided to ask him what the Father actually looked like. My question, in all honesty, was more baiting than sincere. See, I'd read scriptures like, "No one has seen God at any time" (1 John 4:12) and "You cannot see My face, for no man can see Me and live!" (Exod. 33:20). I didn't quite believe the narrative Jonny was feeding us, so in my youthful arrogance I was testing him. I fancied myself a theologian of sorts, and I was on a mission to stump the teacher (much like the Pharisees with Jesus, and it didn't turn out well for them).

Jonny gave me some supermystical answer like, "Well, I don't see His face per se; it's more of a feeling or a general sense of His nearness." Needless to say, I wasn't convinced. But this set me on a journey—to either discover the face of God for myself or disprove the possibility of seeing it altogether. In my heart, though I barely made room for it to be real, I longed to know the God who smiled instead of scowled.

I'll admit, the journey was painfully slow going at first. It felt as if I were continually asking but nothing was happening. McDonald's and Starbucks have trained me to expect immediate results. I place my order, and they give me what I want, right? But I quickly realized that God doesn't work like that.

The process was gradual, like the slow blooming of a flower, but I did start to see God in my everyday life.

I found Him in my children's laughter, in my wife's eyes, in the morning call of a robin on an otherwise dreary day, in the sunset at golden hour, in the reflection of the trees on a still lake in the dead of winter. He seemed to show up everywhere, and in all of it I could hear Him whisper, "I love you." It wasn't written in gigantic neon letters like I thought it'd be; I had to lean in to see it and hear it.

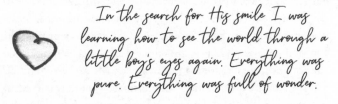

In the search for His smile I was learning how to see the world through a little boy's eyes again. Everything was pure. Everything was full of wonder.

In this yearlong season of awakening, my eyes were opened to His kindness in the ordinary places, in the familiar things, as if He were saying, "See, I did all of this for you." I was Peter Banning in the movie *Hook*, slowly remembering that beneath all the wrinkles, jadedness, and fatigue, I was Peter Pan. I could see the angels in heaven exclaiming, "You're doing it, Cory! You're playing again!" I was coming back to life.

I believe that to see the smile of God, we've got to become kids again. Because the truth is, I don't think God takes much pleasure in a mass of busy adults in a busy world going about their busy lives all in the name of making something of themselves. He's delighted in children, unencumbered by the cares of this world, frolicking through the fields of His goodness as they're meant to do. Matthew 18:2–3 (NIV) says, "He called a little child to him, and placed the child among them. And he said, 'Truly I tell you, unless you change and become like little children, you will never enter the kingdom of heaven.'" In the search for His smile I was learning how to see the world through a little boy's eyes again. Everything was pure. Everything was full of wonder.

It was during this year of rebirth that the refrain of "Reckless Love" was written. I could see the lyrics "O the overwhelming, never-ending, reckless love of God" painted in bright, shining Technicolor over all the dullness and dross that used to drape over the miracle of my life. Everything was made new as I saw His smile over me. Things that used to evoke pain and sorrow found new meaning in its brightness. It was as if He was rewriting the story of my life from beginning to end—the story once penned by a cruel, disappointed old man, now reimagined and revised by the quill of a patient, loving Father. I remembered what it was like to be a kid again, to be held, carefree in the care of God.

So my charge to you is this: Could you ask Him to show you His smile, to show you what He really thinks about you? And when He begins to answer, could you work up the courage to go with Him on the journey? And when you're in the middle of it and it feels slow and awkward and painful, could you press in despite all of it? He loves you more than words can tell.

Going Deeper

A smile is a simple thing. It costs nothing, but it pays big rewards. No matter how you're dressed or whether you're having a good hair day or a bad one, your looks will always be improved with a smile. Smiles are contagious too. Try smiling big at strangers and see what happens! Moods are lifted, joy is released, and everything changes.

+ How we long to have Jesus smile at us. All would be right with the world if that happened, right? Well, think about this: What if Jesus always has been smiling at you?

+ When you close your eyes and picture Jesus, what is the look on His face?

I pray that the look you saw on Jesus' face for you was a smile. If it wasn't, then start the journey as I did by asking Him to help you get to know Him as this delightful God who loves you. Stick with the journey through the slow times because, I can promise you, it will be worth it when you see God's smiles everywhere, as I did.

May God bless you and give you favor on this journey to know His reckless love in greater measure.

NOTES

Day 1—Is God's Love Reckless?

1. Jacqueline Howard, "A 'Wake-Up Call' About What's Killing America's Young People," June 1, 2018, CNN, https://www.cnn.com/2018/06/01/health/youth-injury-death-rate-cdc-study/index.html.

2. A. W. Tozer, *The Pursuit of God* (n.p.: Loki's Publishing, 2017), 10, https://www.amazon.com/Pursuit-God-W-Tozer/dp/1636000886.

3. Cory Asbury, "Beautiful thoughts from my friend, Glenn Packiam regarding #recklesslove. Please enjoy," Facebook, February 1, 2018, https://www.facebook.com/coryasburymusic/photos/a.10153437082065171/10160093480365171/?type=3&theater.

Day 3—Either He's Good, or He Isn't

1. Bill Johnson, *God Is Good: He's Better Than You Think* (Shippensburg, PA: Destiny Image, 2018), https://books.google.com/books?id=0fBGDwAAQBAJ&.

Day 6—The Cost of the Cross (Part 1)

1. Mark Whitehead, *A Daily Walk: A Collection of Quiet Times With Jesus, New Testament: Volume I, The Gospels and Acts* (n.p.: Lulu.com, 2017), 85, https://www.google.com/books/edition/_/qDdFDwAAQBAJ?hl.

Day 7—The Cost of the Cross (Part 2)

1. Isaac Watts, "When I Survey the Wondrous Cross," https://songselect.ccli.com/search/results?List=publicdomain.

Day 11—Who Do You Say I Am?

1. A. W. Tozer, *The Knowledge of the Holy: The Attributes of God, Their Meaning in the Christian Life* (San Francisco: Harper & Row, 1978, 1961), 3–4.

2. Bill Johnson, *God Is Good.*

3. C. S. Lewis, *The Lion, the Witch and the Wardrobe* (New York: HarperCollins, 1994), 80.

Day 15—Can't Earn It, Don't Deserve It

1. Blue Letter Bible, s.v. *"skybalon,"* accessed October 3, 2019, https://www.blueletterbible.org/lang/lexicon/lexicon.cfm?Strongs=G4657&t=KJV.

Day 19—You Are "The One"

1. Goodreads, "Rich Mullins," accessed October 5, 2019, https://www.goodreads.com/quotes/121302-i-grew-up-hearing-everyone-tell-me-god-loves-you.

Day 20—Stop Doing and Start Being

1. Mike Bickle, "Encountering the Father Heart of God: A Vision To Go Deep in God," IHOP Kansas City, https://ihopkcorg-a.akamaihd.net/platform/IHOP/827/307/20070427_Encountering_the_Father_Heart_of_God_Vision_to_Go_Deep_in_God_Mike_Bickle.pdf, 1.

Day 35—"Forgive Us *as We Forgive*"

1. Lewis B. Smedes, *Forgive and Forget: Healing Hurts We Don't Deserve* (New York: HarperCollins, 1996), x.

Day 37—Run Back to the Father

1. *Oxford English Dictionary,* s.v. "prodigal," accessed October 5, 2019, www.oxforddictionaries.com/definition/prodigal.

2. *Oxford English Dictionary,* s.v. "prodigal."

3. Timothy Keller, *The Prodigal God* (New York: Riverhead Books, 2008) xix–xx.

DAY 39—READY TO ENCOUNTER GOD'S RECKLESS LOVE

1. Blue Letter Bible, s.v. *"krataioō,"* accessed October 3, 2019, https://www.blueletterbible.org/lang/lexicon/lexicon.cfm?Strongs=G2901&t=KJV.

ABOUT THE AUTHOR

*C*ORY ASBURY IS a worship leader and songwriter who hails from the mountains of North Carolina. He is also an artist with the Bethel Music Collective, a group who exists to gather, inspire, and encourage the global church toward deeper intimacy with the Father.

His latest album, *Reckless Love*, was Billboard's #1 Christian Album in 2018. Cory has also won three GMA Dove Awards, two K-Love Fan Awards, and the ASCAP Christian Song of the Year Award. In addition he's received three Billboard Music nominations.

The song "Reckless Love" as well as the book you now hold were inspired by Cory's journey into the depths of the Father's heart. Through the birth of his first son and the near-loss of his first daughter, Cory's understanding of the love of God has grown real-life roots. In becoming a father, he truly learned how to be a son.

Fueled by a passion to lead others into their own authentic encounters with God, Cory's ministry is marked by rich spontaneous moments in His presence. He and his wife, Anna, have four beautiful children—Gabriel, Lily, River, and Willow-Grace. To learn more, visit coryasbury.com.

My **FREE GIFT** to You

Dear Reader,

I am so happy you read my book. I hope this book deepened your understanding of God's love for you.

As My Way of Saying *Thank You*...

I am offering you a gift:

Ebook: *One Minute Insights: How to Make Great Choices, Live With Passion, and Get It Right*

To get this **FREE GIFT**, please go to:

www.RecklessLoveBook.com/gift

Thanks again and God bless you,

Cory Asbury